MW01116028

The Ultimate Beginner's Guide to Generative AI

A Step-By-Step Understanding of Fundamental Concepts with Practical Applications, Including Ethical and Societal Impacts

Maxwell T. Sterling, Sr.

Maxwell T. Sterling, Jr.

Copyright © 2024 Maxwell T. Sterling, Sr. All rights reserved.

The content within this book may not be reproduced, duplicated, or transmitted without direct written permission from the author or the publisher.

Under no circumstances will any blame or legal responsibility be held against the publisher, or author, for any damages, reparation, or monetary loss due to the information contained within this book, either directly or indirectly.

Legal Notice:

This book is copyright protected. It is only for personal use. You cannot amend, distribute, sell, use, quote, or paraphrase any part of the content within this book, without the consent of the author or publisher.

Disclaimer Notice:

Please note the information contained within this document is for educational and entertainment purposes only. All effort has been expended to present accurate, up-to-date, reliable, and complete information. No warranties of any kind are declared or implied. Readers acknowledge that the author is not engaged in the rendering of legal, financial, medical, or professional advice. The content within this book has been derived from various sources. Please consult a licensed professional before attempting any techniques outlined in this book.

By reading this document, the reader agrees that under no circumstances is the author responsible for any losses, direct or indirect, that are incurred as a result of the use of the information contained within this document, including, but not limited to, errors, omissions, or inaccuracies.

Contents

Introduction   5

 1. Introduction to Generative AI   9
 2. Core Technologies Behind Generative AI   21
 3. Everyday Uses of Generative AI   45
 4. Generative AI for Personal Productivity   59
 5. Generative AI in Business and Industry   75
 6. Using Generative AI for Educational Purposes   97
 7. Creative Expressions through Generative AI   109
 8. Ethical Considerations and Societal Impact   121
 9. Getting Started with Generative AI Tools   139
10. Global Perspectives on Generative AI   157
11. Navigating the Complexities of AI Ethics   169
12. Community and Collaboration and Keeping Up-To-
    Date   181
13. The Next Frontier: Emerging Trends in AI   197

    Conclusion   219
    Resources   223

INTRODUCTION

AI stands as one of the most transformative technologies of our time, augmenting human capabilities, driving efficiencies, and unlocking unprecedented opportunities across diverse industries.[1]

— SATYA NADELLA, CEO OF MICROSOFT

This powerful endorsement echoes the core message of this book, which aims to unfold the complexities and vast potential of generative artificial intelligence ("AI") for the beginner.

In a bustling hospital in downtown Toronto, University Health Network[2], a machine-learning model analyzes thousands of patient records, predicting health complications before they happen. This transformative technology, called Generative AI, is not confined to

---

1. https://hyscaler.com/insights/microsoft-ceo-satya-nadella-insights-on-ai/
2. https://globalnews.ca/news/9973838/toronto-hospital-network-appoints-chief-ai-scientist/ https://www.uhn.ca/corporate/News/Pages/UHN_becomes_first_Canadian_hospital_to_appoint_Chief_AI_Scientist.aspx

healthcare. It's reshaping industries, enhancing creative processes, and simplifying day-to-day tasks across the globe. Generative AI refers to artificial intelligence systems that can generate new content, from texts and images to code and beyond, based on the data they have been trained on.

This book is crafted with a clear mission: to explain the basics and the complexities of Generative AI to those who have yet to interact with this technology and take those who have interacted further down the path of understanding. Whether you are a small business owner curious about AI, a parent interested in the technological world your children are growing into, or simply an enthusiastic learner, this guide is for you. Our aim is not just to inform you but to make you comfortable and excited about the potential of Generative AI in your personal and professional lives.

As a businessman with a business and legal education, I was initially skeptical when my son, an electrical engineering student at a Midwestern University, introduced me to ChatGPT.

Despite his enthusiasm—claiming it would "revolutionize the planet"—the technology sat unused. However, during a conversation about drafting a complaint letter to an airline, he suggested I try ChatGPT. Reluctantly, I agreed. Surprisingly, the tool crafted a compelling letter and saved me 45 minutes of drafting and revising. That moment was a revelation for me.

Motivated by this experience, I learned more about the potential of generative AI, exploring its practical applications in daily life. This book is a joint effort between my son and me. He brought his technical expertise to the chapters on technology, and we both focused on real-world applications, and I compiled our insights. Writing and editing this book has been a labor of love, fueled by a desire to ease your adventure up the steep learning curve of modern AI technologies.

This book's structure is designed to be a roadmap through Generative AI. Starting with the basics, we'll explore how these systems are built and how they learn. From there, we'll examine real-world applications and dive into the ethical considerations that must guide the use of this powerful tool. I'll provide practical insights on how you can implement Generative AI in various aspects of your life and work, backed by detailed case studies and actionable advice.

Setting the right expectations is crucial. You can look forward to thoroughly understanding Generative AI and practical insights to apply this knowledge. Ethical considerations will be woven throughout our discussions, ensuring you're prepared to use AI responsibly. Interactive elements throughout the book will engage you directly with the material, empowering you with the needed knowledge.

Let me address some common misconceptions for skeptics and curious readers: Generative AI does not aim to replace human jobs, nor is it an uncontrollable force. Throughout this book, particularly in the sections on societal impact and ethical considerations, we'll debunk these myths and more, presenting a balanced view of AI's capabilities and limitations.

For instance, consider the earlier example of AI in healthcare. This technology does not replace doctors but augments their capabilities, allowing them to make more informed decisions faster. This is just one of the many ways that Generative AI is proving to be a beneficial ally in our everyday lives.

As we begin this exploration together, we invite you to approach this book with an open mind and a curious heart. Generative AI's potential is immense, marking the dawn of a transformative era in technology. Understanding its basics is the key to using it responsibly and effectively.

Now, let us embark on this enlightening adventure together. Step by step, we will uncover the myriad ways in which Generative AI seamlessly integrates into and profoundly enriches different aspects of your daily life. From simplifying complex tasks to sparking creativity and decision-making, we'll explore the transformative potential of Generative AI to elevate your personal and professional experiences.

1. INTRODUCTION TO GENERATIVE AI

Generative AI has significantly shifted from being a mere technological experiment to becoming a deeply integrated part of our digital experiences. It is enhancing how we interact with m fundamentally reshaping our creative and cultural landscapes.

— HENRY AJDER

Netflix[1] has revolutionized how we interact with digital content. Using a form of artificial intelligence known as Generative AI, they have developed a platform that suggests movies based on your previous watching patterns and customizes trailers according to your emotional reactions, which are tracked in real-time. This scenario isn't from a futuristic novel; it's a real-world

---

1. www.netflix.com Netflix, Inc. www.netflix.com Netflix, Inc. (2023). How Netflix's Recommendations System Works. Retrieved from https://help.netflix.com/en/node/100639https://help.netflix.com/en/node/100639

application of Generative AI, a technology rapidly becoming a cornerstone in our interaction with the digital world.

Generative AI stands out in technology for its ability to create something new out of something old. It doesn't just analyze data; it uses that data to generate new pieces of information that didn't exist before, from artwork and music to strategic business models and beyond. This ability makes it a powerful tool across various sectors, fundamentally altering how we approach problems and design solutions.

What is Generative AI? Understanding the Basics

Generative AI refers to artificial intelligence technologies that generate new data or content that mimics the training data but is distinctly unique. This kind of AI operates through algorithms that learn from vast amounts of existing data, identify underlying patterns and features, and use this knowledge to produce new, similar data instances. The capability to create sets Generative AI apart from traditional AI systems, which are predominantly focused on analyzing and drawing insights from data rather than creating new output.

The core mechanism underpinning Generative AI involves sophisticated neural networks and learning models that meticulously analyze and interpret extensive datasets. These AI systems harness the power of deep learning to discern intricate patterns within the data, enabling them to generate new, original content that mirrors the complexity and variability of their training inputs. For example, in healthcare, Generative AI algorithms sift through vast patient records to forecast health outcomes or augment diagnostic procedures with remarkable precision. These models are adept at identifying subtle health trends and correlations, offering insights that can significantly enhance patient care and treatment strategies.

The applications of Generative AI extend far and wide, demonstrating a remarkable capacity to revolutionize various industries. In the entertainment sector, it plays a pivotal role in crafting innovative music compositions and dynamic video game environments that cater specifically to the unique preferences of individual users. This personalized approach enriches the user experience, making digital interactions more engaging and satisfying. Meanwhile, in the customer service sector, AI-powered chatbots equipped with Generative AI capabilities are transformational. These chatbots deliver human-like interactions, providing round-the-clock support to customers worldwide. Their ability to understand and respond to customer inquiries with contextually relevant and coherent answers showcases the profound impact of Generative AI on enhancing service efficiency and user satisfaction.

Understanding Generative AI transcends the technical intricacies of its operation. It involves appreciating its vast potential to spur innovation across an array of life's facets. As we further investigate this technology, it becomes evident that its importance lies in its ability to replicate human-like outputs and its innovative prowess. Generative AI stands at the edge of technological advancement, offering novel solutions to complex problems and enriching our lives unimaginably. By familiarizing ourselves with these concepts, we unveil the myriad ways in which Generative AI can influence and improve our personal and professional endeavors. This exploration encourages us to envision a future where Generative AI seamlessly integrates into the fabric of our daily lives, unlocking new possibilities for growth, creativity, and efficiency.

THE EVOLUTION OF GENERATIVE AI: FROM CONCEPT TO EVERYDAY USE

The story of Generative AI is not just a narrative of technological evolution; it is a profound testament to human ingenuity and the relentless pursuit of knowledge. The exploration from the theoretical underpinnings of artificial intelligence to the sophisticated Generative AI applications we see today offers a fascinating glimpse into the rapid advancements that have shaped this field. Initially rooted in the foundational theories of machine learning and neural networks, the development of Generative AI began as an ambitious attempt to mimic the human brain's ability to generate new ideas and solutions.

Historically, the concept of artificial intelligence has been a topic of both scientific inquiry and philosophical speculation. The initial breakthrough came with the realization that machines could be taught to learn from data, a fundamental principle that paved the way for all future developments in AI. However, the introduction of neural networks genuinely set the stage for the emergence of Generative AI. These networks, designed to simulate the interconnected neuron structures in the human brain, became the backbone of the most advanced AI systems, enabling them to evaluate and learn from large datasets and generate new content that mimics the input data in creative ways.

Several vital breakthroughs have marked the milestones in Generative AI, each propelling the field forward significantly. Introducing models like Google's BERT and OpenAI's GPT series revolutionized natural language processing, allowing machines to understand and generate human-like text with remarkable accuracy. BERT (Bidirectional Encoder Representations from Transformers) helped computers grasp the context of words in a sentence more effectively than ever before, enhancing the quality and applicability of machine-generated text. Following BERT, the GPT series pushed the boundaries further, with GPT-3 and the subsequent GPT-4 introducing enhanced language comprehension and generation capabilities. Now, the new GPT 4o will further enhance the processing. These models did not just understand the text; they could write poems, draft articles, and even code, showcasing an unprecedented linguistic and cognitive ability.

The societal and technological impacts of these developments have been transformative. Generative AI has been used in sectors like healthcare to predict patient diagnoses and treatments, significantly improving outcomes and efficiency. In entertainment, AI-driven tools have created personalized content, offering recommendations and experiences uniquely tailored to individual preferences. The technology's ability to automate and enhance creative processes has also democratized creativity, enabling individuals without professional skills to generate professional-level designs, artworks, and written content.

Industries have adopted Generative AI to optimize operations, innovate products, and enhance customer engagement. From finance, where AI models predict market trends and automate trading, to customer service, where chatbots handle inquiries with increasing empathy and understanding, the applications are as diverse as they are impactful. The integration of Generative AI has improved efficiency and sparked a wave of innovation in product development and business strategies.

Looking ahead, the future directions of Generative AI appear boundless. The ongoing research aims to make these systems more autonomous and ethical, reducing their dependency on vast data inputs and ensuring their decisions are fair and unbiased. As AI continues to evolve, its potential to further revolutionize industries and influence our daily lives remains a compelling narrative of progress and possibility.

In reflecting on these advancements, it becomes clear that Generative AI is more than just a technological tool; it is a dynamic and evolving field that continues to challenge our ideas about what machines can achieve. The case studies of technologies like BERT

and GPT-3

demonstrate the rapid progression in AI capabilities and highlight the collaborative effort of thousands of researchers and developers dedicated to advancing this frontier of science. As we stand on the brink of discoveries, the adventure of Generative AI continues to unfold, promising to reshape our world in ways we are just beginning to imagine.

How Generative AI is Different from Other AI Technologies

AI is vast and varied, with each technology designed to address specific problems or enhance certain tasks. Traditional AI, often called analytical AI, is adept at managing and examining extensive data sets to discern patterns, forecast outcomes, or offer insights. These systems are fundamentally designed to enhance decision-making processes in business, science, and daily life. For instance, analytical AI can scan through extensive financial records to identify fraudulent activities or optimize logistics by predicting the best routes for delivery trucks. The primary role of these systems is to analyze existing information and provide actionable insights based on that analysis.

In contrast, Generative AI introduces a novel dimension to artificial intelligence by not just analyzing data but creating new data that did not exist. This capability to generate new content—from realistic images and music to complex written prose and code—marks a significant departure from traditional AI's capabilities. Generative AI uses foundational technologies such as neural networks and deep learning but leverages them to innovate rather than interpret. For example, while a traditional AI model might analyze customer data to predict purchasing behaviors, a Generative AI model could create personalized marketing content tailored to individual consumer profiles, engaging customers in a personal and direct way.

The innovative applications of Generative AI are broad and profoundly transformative. In drug discovery, for example, Generative AI models expedite the creation of new drug molecules with desired properties by learning from vast databases of known chemical compounds. Generative AI speeds up the research process and reduces the costs and risks associated with drug development. In creative industries, Generative AI is used to design unique fashion pieces by learning from current trends and historical fashion data, offering designers a powerful tool to explore new styles and ideas that might not have been conceived otherwise.

However, the capabilities that set Generative AI apart also introduce unique challenges and ethical considerations. One of the primary concerns is the potential for misuse, such as creating deepfakes, which are realistic but entirely fabricated audiovisual content that can be used to mislead or harm. As Generative AI becomes more sophisticated, distinguishing between actual and generated content becomes increasingly complex, posing significant risks in contexts ranging from politics to personal relationships. Furthermore, the autonomy of Generative AI in creating content also raises questions about intellectual property rights and the originality of AI-generated works, complicating legal frameworks that need to be designed to consider the creative capabilities of machines.

Looking to the future, the potential of Generative AI to influence technological developments is profound. As these systems become more integrated into various sectors, they could fundamentally alter how we produce goods, interact with technology, and understand creativity. There is a pressing need for robust ethical guidelines and legislative frameworks to ensure that the deployment of Generative AI technologies benefits society. The evolution of Generative AI could lead to more personalized and engaging educational tools, revolutionize design and manufacturing processes, and even alter how we interact with the digital world through more immersive and interactive AI-driven environments.

Considering these considerations, it's clear that Generative AI does not merely extend the capacities of traditional analytical AI but introduces an entirely new framework for interaction between humans and machines. As we continue to explore the possibilities of this exciting technology, it is crucial to foster an informed and ethical approach to its development and use, ensuring that Generative AI serves as a tool for positive transformation and creative enhancement across all areas of human endeavor.

THE TERMINOLOGY OF AI

Navigating AI often begins with understanding the terminology that forms the backbone of discussions and literature on the subject. For anyone stepping into this field, especially those who have not interacted with AI before, grasping these terms is akin to learning the basic rules of a new language. Here, we revisit and clarify some of the critical terms you've encountered in this chapter, aiming to solidify your understanding and prepare you for deeper engagement with AI concepts.

Artificial Intelligence (AI): Artificial Intelligence represents the broader discipline within computer science focused on creating systems capable of performing tasks that typically require human intelligence. This encompasses various capabilities such as understanding natural language, recognizing patterns and images, making decisions, and solving complex problems. At its heart, AI aims to mimic or replicate human cognitive functions, making it a cornerstone concept in generative technologies. The pursuit of AI spans the development of simple algorithms for specific tasks to the creation of advanced systems that learn and adapt over time. Generative AI, a subset of artificial intelligence, specifically focuses on generating new content, whether text, images, or even code, like what a human might produce. This facet of AI is particularly revolutionary as it moves beyond the traditional scope of understanding and responding to input, venturing into the new frontier of creativity and innovation traditionally thought to be exclusive to human intellect.

Understanding AI in this broad sense is essential, as it lays the foundation for exploring the more specialized areas of machine learning, deep learning, and their applications in generating dynamic and intelligent systems. Through this lens, AI is not just a tool for automating tasks but a transformative technology that continually reshapes our approach to problem-solving and creative expression.

Neural Networks: At its core, a neural network in AI is an architecture modeled loosely after the human brain. It consists of layers of nodes, or 'neurons,' each designed to perform specific computations. These neurons are interconnected in a way that allows them to transmit signals to one another, like the synaptic connections in the human brain. When a neural network begins a task, it processes the input data through these interconnected layers, each making its calculations and passing on the results. Neural networks possess a remarkable capability to extract knowledge from the data they handle. By adjusting the strength of the neuron connections between neurons (a process known as 'weight adjustment'), the network optimizes its internal settings to produce the most accurate output possible based on the input it receives. This learning process is central to AI's ability to perform tasks ranging from recognizing faces in photos to predicting stock market trends.

Machine Learning: This term pertains to a technique for analyzing data that automates the development of analytical models. Machine learning is an artificial intelligence that enables computers to make decisions based on data and learn autonomously. Machine learning allows systems to enhance task efficiency over time without direct programming. The learning process involves algorithms discovering patterns and features in the data they analyze. As the system encounters new data, these algorithms allow it to adjust and refine its approach to achieve better accuracy. Machine learning is ubiquitous in applications where it's impractical for humans to manually create rules or define behaviors, such as detecting fraudulent credit card transactions or filtering spam emails.

Deep Learning: A subset of machine learning, deep learning utilizes layers of neural networks to analyze various data input factors. What sets deep learning apart is its ability to process data through layers of increasing complexity. In a deep learning model, each network layer extracts different data features, with initial layers learning basic features and deeper layers recognizing more complex patterns. This structure enables deep learning models to handle vast amounts of data and perform highly sophisticated tasks, such as translating languages or generating realistic human speech. Deep learning has been a pivotal force behind many recent advancements in AI, pushing the boundaries of what machines can achieve.

Understanding these foundational concepts is crucial as they recur throughout various discussions on AI. Whether we explore how AI transforms healthcare by predicting diseases or investigating its ability to enhance customer service through chatbots, these terms provide the necessary framework to appreciate the depth and breadth of AI's capabilities.

Moreover, the interplay between these concepts highlights the layered complexity of AI systems and the remarkable ways they mimic human learning and decision-making processes. Neural networks, for instance, provide the structural foundation, machine learning offers the methodology, and deep learning brings the capacity for handling intricately detailed tasks. Together, they enable AI systems to perform assigned tasks and adapt and improve over time, reflecting dynamism and responsiveness that continues to transform industries and everyday life.

As we continue to explore more specialized applications and implications of AI, keeping these definitions in mind will enhance your understanding and ability to engage with the technology critically.

It's not just about recognizing what AI can do; it's about understanding how it does it, which is essential for leveraging its benefits and navigating its challenges effectively. In essence, as we peel back the layers of AI's functionality and potential, we equip ourselves not only with knowledge but also with the foresight to drive innovation responsibly and ethically in the years to come.

2. Core Technologies Behind Generative AI

Innovation is the outcome of a habit, not a random act.[1]

— Sukant Ratnakar

This insight into the chronic nature of innovation underscores the systematic approach behind the development of generative AI technologies. Exploring the intricacies of neural networks and machine learning, it becomes clear that each breakthrough in AI is not merely a stroke of luck but the result of rigorous, systematic exploration and iteration. This chapter seeks to unravel these complex processes, illustrating how structured creativity shapes the cutting edge of AI development.

The further exploration of Generative AI requires the foundational technologies that enable these systems to function and thrive in various applications. The heart of Generative AI lies in its ability to mimic some of the most intricate processes of the human brain, a

---

1. Ratnakar, S. (2021). *Quantraz: A force within*. BecomeShakespeare.com.

feat achieved through advanced neural networks. This chapter aims to decode these complex structures, offering a clear view of how they operate, evolve, and impact the development of AI technologies that are transforming our world.

DECODING NEURAL NETWORKS: THE BUILDING BLOCKS OF GENERATIVE AI

The human brain's architecture inspires neural networks. They are composed of nodes, or neurons, linked like a vast network. Each neuron processes input data, makes simple decisions, and passes on its output to subsequent layers of neurons. The process resembles a relay race in which the baton of information is continuously handed off until the final production emerges. This output could be anything from identifying the face in a photograph to generating the lyrics of a song.

The architecture of neural networks in Generative AI can vary dramatically, each structured to serve different purposes and complexities. The Generative Adversarial Networks ("GANs") are at the heart of these variations, a revolutionary concept where two neural networks compete. Imagine an artist and a critic: one creates and evaluates a work. The artist (the generator) generates new data, while the critic (the discriminator) assesses whether this new data fits the actual data's criteria. This competition drives the generator to produce increasingly realistic outputs, enhancing the AI's creation ability.

As we marvel at GANs' capabilities to produce increasingly realistic outputs, it's crucial to consider the ethical implications of such technology. The realism enabled by GANs raises concerns about their use in creating deceptive media, such as deepfakes, which can be employed to spread misinformation or violate privacy. Developers and stakeholders must implement strict ethical guidelines and transparency measures when deploying these models to mitigate potential misuse.

Further expanding the variety of neural network architectures, Recurrent Neural Networks ("RNNs") and Convolutional Neural Networks ("CNNs") stand out for their specialized abilities to process distinct types of data inputs. RNNs shine in scenarios where understanding the context or sequence of data points is critical. They are designed to handle sequential information, making them perfect for tasks like language translation, where the order of words dramatically influences meaning, or speech recognition, where the sequence of sounds determines the spoken words. Their unique capability to remember and utilize previous inputs in processing current data allows for a nuanced understanding of sequences, which is paramount in accurately predicting the next element in the series.

On the other hand, CNNs are adept at tasks involving spatial hierarchies in data, such as recognizing and interpreting images or videos. This proficiency stems from their structure, which is adept at identifying patterns within a grid, such as the edges, shapes, and textures that compose an object in an image. By dissecting an image into smaller, manageable pieces and analyzing these for patterns, CNNs can comprehensively understand the visual input. This makes them particularly effective in fields like computer vision, where identifying and categorizing visual data is essential.

The distinct operational frameworks of RNNs and CNNs highlight neural networks' versatility in adapting to various data types and tasks. By leveraging these architectures, Generative AI systems can more effectively mimic human-like capabilities in processing and understanding complex, sequential, or spatial data. This diversity in neural network design broadens the applicability of Generative AI across different domains and enhances the sophistication with which these systems can generate realistic, nuanced outputs.

Recent advancements in neural network architectures have pushed the boundaries of what Generative AI can achieve, introducing more sophisticated systems like Capsule Networks and Self-Organizing Maps. Capsule Networks mark a significant evolution in our approach to image recognition tasks. Unlike traditional CNNs that may falter when recognizing objects from new or unusual angles, Capsule Networks excel in identifying objects regardless of their orientation or the perspective from which they're viewed. This capability emerges from their unique structure, designed to capture and maintain the hierarchical relationships between different parts of an object, allowing for a more dynamic and flexible understanding of images. This advancement enhances the system's accuracy in image recognition and paves the way for more intuitive interactions between AI and the three-dimensional world.

On the other hand, Self-Organizing Maps ("SOMs") introduces a novel approach to unsupervised learning and data visualization, distinguishing themselves as invaluable tools in tackling complex problem-solving scenarios where traditional linear methods fall short. SOMs organize data into a map where similar items are positioned closer together, creating a 'map' of input features that can reveal hidden patterns and relationships within vast datasets. This ability to visualize complex data structures makes SOMs particularly useful in fields such as market research, bioinformatics, and more, where understanding the intricate structure of data is crucial.

The training of these neural networks is a meticulous process involving adjusting internal parameters in response to the difference between the output produced and the desired output. This training process is iterative, requiring numerous repetitions through the dataset to gradually refine the network's accuracy. It's akin to a sculptor, who must chip away gradually, assessing after each stroke, to form a desired figure from a block of marble.

Neural networks play a critical role in the functionality of Generative AI systems. They are not just tools for data analysis but are instrumental in creating new, realistic data that can be indistinguishable from actual human-generated data. This capability is at the core of Generative AI's transformative potential across various sectors, from healthcare, where it can predict patient health outcomes, to entertainment, where it can customize content to individual preferences.

While neural networks have transformed industries by enabling the creation of new realistic data, they also pose significant ethical challenges. For instance, biases in training data can lead these networks to propagate stereotypes or unfair decisions, especially in areas like hiring or law enforcement. Addressing these issues requires careful curation of training datasets, ongoing monitoring for biased outcomes, and the development of models that can explain their decisions to human overseers.

The exploration of neural networks offers a profound insight into the operational backbone of Generative AI, revealing these technologies' complexities and immense possibilities. As we continue to navigate the layers of Generative AI applications, understanding these core technologies allows us to appreciate what AI can do and how it does it—empowering us with the knowledge to harness these tools responsibly and innovatively in our personal and professional lives.

Now that we have explored the intricate architecture and potential applications (and misapplications) of neural networks in Generative AI, it's an excellent time to assess your understanding of the material covered. This quiz will help consolidate your knowledge and ensure you grasp the fundamental concepts discussed in this chapter.

Quiz: Understanding the Core Technologies Behind Generative AI

1. What is the primary function of neural networks in Generative AI?

    a. To analyze large datasets for business intelligence
    b. To generate realistic and novel data outputs
    c. To secure data against cyber threats
    d. To manage AI operational costs

2. Generative Adversarial Networks (GANs) consist of which two main components?

    a. Encoder and Decoder
    b. Sensor and Responder
    c. Generator and Discriminator
    d. Optimizer and Evaluator

3. Which type of neural network is especially effective for tasks that involve sequential data like language translation or speech recognition?

    a. Convolutional Neural Networks (CNNs)
    b. Recurrent Neural Networks (RNNs)
    c. Generative Adversarial Networks (GANs)
    d. Transformer Networks

4. What ethical consideration is crucial when deploying Generative AI technologies, especially GANs?

    a. Cost reduction
    b. Speed of computation
    c. Prevention of deceptive uses such as deep fakes
    d. Color accuracy in generated images

5. Describe in your own words how a GAN could be used to improve the realism of virtual environments in video games.

Answer key:

b. To generate realistic and novel data outputs

c. Generator and Discriminator

b Recurrent Neural Networks (RNNs)

c. Prevention of deceptive uses such as deep fakes.

GENERATIVE VS. TRADITIONAL AI: UNDERSTANDING THE DIFFERENCES

When exploring artificial intelligence, one encounters a fundamental bifurcation: Generative AI and traditional AI. Though stemming from the same foundational concepts of machine learning and data processing, these two branches diverge significantly in their functionalities and applications. Traditional AI, often called analytical AI, excels in making sense of data, providing insights, and enhancing decision-making processes. It analyzes existing information to predict outcomes, automate tasks, or detect patterns. This form of AI powers systems like fraud detection algorithms in banking or demand forecasting in supply chain management.

Generative AI, on the other hand, steps beyond analysis to creation. It uses learned patterns from extensive datasets not just to understand or predict but to generate new data that resembles the original input. This could manifest as creating realistic human voices, composing music, or even generating synthetic data for training other AI systems. The distinction here is not merely technical but philosophical, extending AI's role from a passive analyzer to an active creator, thus broadening the scope of its capabilities and applications.

To visualize the operational frameworks of these two AI types, consider a chart where one axis represents data processing capabilities and the other creativity and innovation. Traditional AI would score high on data processing but low on creativity, as its functionalities are primarily confined to interpreting and acting on given data. Generative AI would spread across both axes, showcasing high data processing capabilities and a significant score in creativity, evidenced by its ability to create new, functional pieces of data.

The applications of these AI types also differ markedly based on their capabilities. In predictive analytics, a traditional AI system analyzes historical data to forecast future events, such as predicting stock market trends or customer churn. Such systems thrive on large amounts of existing data, applying learned algorithms to project outcomes. Generative AI, conversely, finds its strength in fields requiring a degree of novelty and customization. For example, in digital marketing, Generative AI can create varied content that adapts to different user interactions, providing personalized experiences that traditional AI would not efficiently generate.

This comparative exploration between Generative and traditional AI highlights the diverse potentials of AI technologies and helps delineate where each can be most effectively employed. Understanding these differences will be crucial in leveraging AI tools for the right tasks as AI evolves, ensuring that technology implementation is strategic and practical.

Finally, as we continue to advance in the field of Generative AI, the ethical use of these powerful technologies remains a paramount concern. Stakeholders must prioritize the development of ethical AI by fostering an interdisciplinary approach that includes ethicists, sociologists, legal experts alongside technologists. This collaboration can ensure that Generative AI serves the public good, enhancing lives while safeguarding against the risks associated with AI-driven decision-making.

IN-DEPTH ANALYSIS OF GENERATIVE ALGORITHMS

In the expansive field of Generative AI, the engines driving innovation are diverse and sophisticated algorithms tailored to specific tasks and challenges. Generative Adversarial Networks ("GANs") stand out for their unique architecture and the compelling way they mimic competitive human interactions to improve their outputs. GANs consist of two parts: the generator and the discriminator. The generator's role is to create indistinguishable data from accurate data, while the discriminator evaluates this data against the actual dataset, trying to identify if it's real or fake. This setup creates a dynamic environment where both networks continually learn and adapt from each other's decisions, driving the generator to produce increasingly accurate outputs.

The training process of GANs involves running both the generator and the discriminator in a loop, where the generator tries to maximize the chances of the discriminator making a mistake, and the discriminator strives to catch the errors of the generator. This method, known as adversarial training, is crucial for developing models that generate highly realistic images, videos, and voice recordings. However, it's not without challenges. Issues such as mode collapse, where the generator starts producing minimal varieties of outputs, and non-convergence, where the generator and discriminator do not stabilize, are common. These problems are addressed through techniques like adding noise to inputs or using different architectures, such as conditional GANs and cycle GANs, designed to enhance stability and output diversity.

Conditional GANs, for example, incorporate additional labels that provide the generator and discriminator with extra information to help guide the learning process. This setup allows for generating more specific items based on conditional data, such as generating photographs of birds when the label specifies a particular bird species. CycleGANs take this a step further by learning to translate an image from one domain to another without paired examples, enabling the conversion of horses to zebras in pictures or the transformation of summer to winter scenes.

Another pivotal algorithm of Generative AI is the Variational Autoencoder ("VAE"). VAEs are designed to create a compressed, encoded representation of data, which can then generate new data items like those in the training set. They work by encoding data into a latent space with defined dimensions and then decoding from this space back to the original data space. VAEs are particularly useful when you need a robust model to handle missing data, generate new data points with variations, or smooth out noisy data inputs.

Diffusion models represent a newer class of generative models that gradually refine a random noise pattern into a sample of coherent data. These models start by learning how to add progressively random noise to training data until the data becomes pure noise. Then, the process is reversed during inference, denoising the random pattern step by step to produce a data sample. This approach is especially effective in generating high-quality images and enhancing the resolution of existing images.

When comparing these algorithms, it becomes evident that each has strengths suited to particular data types and applications. GANs are highly effective in tasks where realism and detail are paramount, such as photorealistic image generation. VAEs offer advantages in applications requiring robust handling of incomplete data sets or generating new data points based on learned distributions. Meanwhile, diffusion models are breaking new ground in the quality of generated images and their applicability in enhancing image resolution.

Ongoing research in these algorithms continues to push the boundaries of what's possible in Generative AI. Innovations such as improving the stability of GAN training, enhancing the efficiency of VAEs, and scaling up diffusion models to handle more complex datasets are on the horizon. These developments promise to improve the capabilities of Generative AI applications and open new possibilities for creative and practical applications across industries. As these technologies evolve, they continue transforming digital content creation, data synthesis, and more, marking an exciting phase of growth and discovery in artificial intelligence.

THE ROLE OF MACHINE LEARNING AND DEEP LEARNING

Machine learning algorithms are not just an integral part of Generative AI; they are its very scaffolding. These algorithms empower Generative AI technologies, enabling them to learn from data, adapt to new inputs, and create data that mimics the original models yet exhibits novel features. Machine learning involves teaching computers to learn from and make decisions based on the data they process. This capability is foundational for any AI system that aims to generate new content because it allows it to understand and mimic complex patterns and relationships within the data.

Deep learning, a subset of machine learning represented by layers of algorithms called neural networks, pushes this capability further. It allows Generative AI systems to handle and interpret immensely complex data sets with a finesse that mimics human intuition. Each layer of a deep learning model processes an aspect of the data, refines it, and passes it on to the next, gradually extracting and refining features. By the time the data has passed through all the layers, the system has a detailed and nuanced understanding of it, enabling the generation of new content that is contextually rich and varied. This depth of processing is crucial for tasks like creating realistic human speech or generating detailed visual images that look real and are filled with contextually appropriate elements.

The evolution of these algorithms over the years has significantly enhanced the capabilities of Generative AI. Early machine learning models could categorize and predict based on clear, simple patterns in modest data sets. As these models evolved into more complex neural networks, their ability to process and generate complex patterns has dramatically improved. Today's deep learning networks can develop everything from convincing articles and music pieces to strategic business recommendations, adapting their real-time output to reflect new data inputs.

In practical terms, applying these technologies in real-world Generative AI applications is both broad and profound. In the media sector, for instance, deep learning models analyze current trends and viewer feedback to generate new script ideas or music that is likely to be popular. In the automotive industry, machine learning algorithms digest large data sets from vehicle sensors to predict and automate maintenance processes, thus not only saving costs but also preventing accidents by addressing mechanical problems proactively.

These examples demonstrate the capability of machine learning and deep learning to drive Generative AI applications and their potential to transform industry operations. By automating the creative and analytical processes, these technologies allow for scalability and personalization that was previously unattainable. Whether customizing media content for individual preferences or optimizing industrial processes based on predictive analytics, the implications of these technologies stretch across all sectors, heralding a new era of efficiency and innovation powered by Generative AI.

How Generative AI Models Are Trained: Simplified

Understanding how Generative AI models are trained can be likened to learning how a chef masters cooking. Just as a chef uses various ingredients to create a dish, Generative AI models use data to generate new content. The process begins quite simply: the model is fed data, learns from this data, and then uses what it has learned to create new, similar data. This learning process is iterative, meaning it repeats, gradually improving AI's ability to produce accurate, high-quality outputs. Each cycle through the data enhances the model's 'understanding,' refining its capabilities.

The ingredients are diverse data forms—images, text, audio, and more. The quality, volume, and diversity of this data are crucial. High-quality data are like premium ingredients, ensuring the information the AI learns from is accurate and representative. Volume pertains to the quantity of data; more data provides the AI with more examples to learn from, which typically leads to better performance. Diversity in data helps the model learn to handle a wide range of scenarios, preventing it from producing results that are too narrow or biased toward a particular characteristic. This diversity is significant because it shapes the AI's behavior and output, ensuring that the AI can perform well across different tasks and environments.

Training an AI model has its challenges. Overfitting, for instance, occurs when a model learns the details and there is noise in the training data to the extent that it negatively impacts the model's performance on new data. This is like a student memorizing answers instead of understanding the subject. On the other hand, underfitting happens when a model is too simple to learn the underlying pattern of the data, much like a chef who needs to know more techniques to handle a complex recipe. Data bias, where the training data does not represent the real-world scenarios the model will encounter, can lead the AI to make incorrect or unethical decisions. Finally, the computational intensity of training large models with vast amounts of data requires significant computational resources, which can be costly and time-consuming.

In real-world applications, the training of Generative AI models is evident in sectors like healthcare and customer service. AI models are trained on diverse medical images to predict patient diagnoses in healthcare. These models learn to recognize patterns in the data indicative of specific health conditions, enabling doctors to diagnose diseases from images such as X-rays or MRIs. For instance, a model trained on dermatological images can learn to distinguish between benign moles and malignant melanomas, providing a valuable tool for dermatologists.

In customer service, chatbots trained on vast datasets of customer interaction data can simulate human-like conversations. These AI systems learn from previous customer service interactions and are continually updated with new interactions, enhancing their ability to handle various customer queries. The training process involves understanding the text of customer interactions and the nuances of human communication, such as intent and emotion, enabling these chatbots to provide accurate and contextually appropriate responses.

Training Generative AI models is a complex yet fascinating process at the heart of their functionality. By understanding how these models are trained, you can better appreciate their capabilities and the intricacies involved in their development. This knowledge explains how AI creates new content and highlights the importance of careful, ethical training practices to ensure that AI systems perform effectively and fairly. The applications and implications of these technologies, remember that their output relies heavily on the effectiveness of their training, underscoring the need for rigorous standards and diverse datasets in developing Generative AI.

NATURAL LANGUAGE PROCESSING: MAKING AI UNDERSTAND US

Natural Language Processing ("NLP") is a critical subset of Generative AI tasked with bridging the communication gap between human language and machine interpretation. Its role is pivotal: to enable machines to understand and interact in human-like language, facilitating a seamless exchange of information. NLP equips Generative AI with the ability to parse, comprehend, and even generate text that mirrors human conversational patterns, thereby expanding AI's utility across various applications, from automated customer service agents to sophisticated content generation systems.

The techniques utilized in NLP are diverse and intricate, reflecting the complexity of human language. Tokenization, for example, breaks down text into smaller, manageable pieces, such as words or phrases, which are more accessible for the machine to process. Sentiment analysis allows AI to detect the emotional tone behind words, enabling it to respond appropriately in interactions. This could range from detecting customer dissatisfaction in a service interaction to understanding the mood of a social media post. Language models like Generative Pre-trained Transformer ("GPT") represent the pinnacle of NLP's capabilities. These models, trained on vast text datasets, can generate coherent, contextually relevant text based on their input. Their training involves adjusting millions of parameters to reflect language usage, style, and grammar nuances, making them potent tools for generating human-like text.

Despite these advancements, NLP has its challenges. The complexity of human language, idioms, sarcasm, and cultural nuances often eludes even the most sophisticated AI systems. Teaching machines to interpret and generate human language involves processing vast amounts of text data and understanding the context and subtext that can drastically alter meanings. For instance, the same word can have different meanings in different contexts—a challenge NLP systems are still learning to navigate effectively.

Looking towards the future, the trajectory of NLP within Generative AI is geared towards even greater sophistication. Advances in machine learning, especially in deep learning, are continually refining the ability of NLP systems to understand and interact with human language with greater accuracy. Future developments may allow NLP systems to master multilingual communication, enabling seamless interactions across language barriers without human translators. Additionally, as these systems become more adept at context recognition, we can expect a new generation of AI assistants who understand our words and the intent and emotion behind them, making interactions more natural and intuitive.

The potential of NLP to enhance the capabilities of Generative AI is immense. As we navigate the complexities and challenges of teaching machines the subtleties of human language, the horizon of what's possible expands. From creating more engaging and personalized user experiences to breaking down language barriers, NLP stands at the forefront of making AI a tool of computation and a communication partner. As we continue to refine these technologies, the promise of AI that can truly understand and interact with us in our language is not just a remote possibility but a forthcoming reality.

LEADING GENERATIVE AI MODELS

Understanding Generative AI models is akin to surveying the most advanced tools in a rapidly evolving field. These models are not just technological advancements; they represent benchmarks in AI capabilities, setting standards and pushing boundaries in various applications, from natural language processing to artistic creation. Recognizing and analyzing these models is crucial for anyone looking to grasp AI's current capabilities and anticipate its trajectory.

The significance of such benchmarking lies in its dual role: It showcases what is currently possible with AI and highlights areas ripe for future development. By studying these models, developers, researchers, and users can learn to appreciate the strengths and limitations of current AI technologies. This will enable them to apply AI solutions and innovate more effectively and strategically.

Interactive Learning through Exploration

To deepen your understanding of how these AI models operate and affect outputs, consider engaging with the following interactive exercises:

Exercise 1: Exploring Neural Networks with an Online Simulator

Explore the intricacies of neural network architecture using an online simulator. This exercise allows you to adjust the number of layers in a neural network and observe the variations in output. By modifying the layers, you can see firsthand how each change impacts the network's learning and output accuracy, providing practical insight into the architectural dependencies of AI models.

Exercise 2: Generative Text with GPT-3

Experience the capabilities of GPT-3, a state-of-the-art language model by OpenAI, by prompting it to generate a short story about a lost robot. Modify your input prompts to experiment with different styles and tones and observe how the AI interprets and responds to these variations. This exercise demonstrates advanced NLP models' adaptability and creative potential in generating diverse content.

Exercise 3: Creating Art with DALL-E 2

Utilize DALL-E 2 to create a detailed image of a futuristic cityscape at sunset. Specify elements like flying cars and towering skyscrapers to see how the AI incorporates these details into a cohesive visual representation. This activity allows you to engage with cutting-edge image generation technology and encourages you to reflect on how varying descriptions influence AI-generated artwork.

Overview of Top Generative AI Models

In generative AI, we must highlight the trailblazers and innovative newcomers shaping this dynamic field. Notably, GPT-3 and DALL-E2 from OpenAI have set significant benchmarks in natural language processing and image generation. The arena continues to expand with advancements like ChatGPT 4 and GPT-4o, pushing conversational AI's boundaries.

ChatGPT has revolutionized how machines comprehend and participate in human-like dialogues. It enhances responsiveness and relevance in real-time interactions, becoming a critical asset in sectors like customer service—where accurate responses are crucial—and education, which benefits from personalized learning experiences.

GPT-4o, building on previous achievements, elevates these conversational abilities with a deeper understanding of context and text subtleties. Its advanced text generation capabilities make it invaluable for developing engaging learning materials across various sectors, such as legal, drafting and reviewing documents, and education. Creative writing facilitates the exploration of new styles and ideas with ease.

Adding to this list, other notable platforms include:

BERT and **T5 from Google**

excel at understanding and generating human language. BERT is pivotal for enhancing search engine results by understanding natural language queries, while T5 adapts to various language tasks without needing task-specific data training.

DeepMind's AlphaCode

excels in writing computer programs, demonstrating proficiency in coding competitions. This model showcases AI's potential in automating complex problem-solving tasks in software development.

Meta AI's **BlenderBot**

is remarkable for its engagement in more personable and lengthy conversations, pushing chatbots' capabilities to provide more relatable and context-aware interactions.

MidJourney

and Stable Diffusion

focus on visual creativity, offering tools that convert textual descriptions into high-quality artistic visuals. These models are particularly adept at aiding designers and artists in visualizing ideas and concepts efficiently and with stunning detail.

Each model contributes uniquely to the generative AI field, showcasing a rich diversity of capabilities from textual to visual AI applications. This highlights generative AI's broad applicability and emphasizes its potential to inspire innovation across various mediums.

Together, these models demonstrate the rapid advancements in AI, continually redefining the limits of what AI can achieve. They offer a glimpse into a future where AI assists, enhances, and inspires human creativity across all aspects of life.

Comparative Analysis and Impact Assessment

Comparing these models reveals underlying technologies, applications, and performance differences. For instance, the way GPT-3 handles language nuances might be more advanced than earlier models. However, DALL-E's capacity to generate complex images from textual descriptions showcases technological advancement. These models collectively represent the cutting edge of AI capabilities, driving innovations that influence other technologies and sectors.

Evaluating their impact, it's clear that these AI models have advanced the field technically and raised important considerations regarding AI ethics, data privacy, and the future of work. Their development and deployment continue to spark debates and discussions shaping AI's regulatory and ethical environments.

Future Prospects

Looking ahead, the evolution of these leading models suggests a trajectory toward even more integrated, intuitive, and ethically aware AI systems. The potential emergence of models seamlessly combining text, voice, and visual capabilities could redefine multi-media interactions. At the same time, advancements in AI ethics aim to ensure that these technologies contribute positively to society.

The exploration of these leading Generative AI models highlights the remarkable capabilities of modern AI and underscores the ongoing need for innovation, responsible use, and ethical consideration. As we transition to the next chapter, which examines the practical applications and moral dimensions of these technologies, we carry forward not just an understanding of what AI can do but a vision of what it should do, fostering a future where technology amplifies creativity, enhances productivity, and upholds our shared values.

3. Everyday Uses of Generative AI

*Generative AI allows us to turn our imagination into reality—
when done well, this feels nothing short of magic.*[1]

— Andreessen Horowitz

This quote from Andreessen Horowitz highlights the transformative power of generative AI. This technology uses algorithms to create new, unique content based on existing data in content creation and the groundbreaking changes it brings to everyday digital interactions.

Generative AI is increasingly making its mark in our daily lives, especially digital ones. For instance, on social media platforms, the technology suggests friends to connect with or shows ads for products you might be interested in. In online shopping, the technology recommends products based on your browsing history or shows you items like the ones you're looking at. This technology is quietly

---

1. https://a16z.com/generative-ai-the-next-consumer-platform/

weaving its way through our interactions and shaping the personalized content that seems to know what we like, sometimes before we do it ourselves. AI's role in transforming our digital experiences is multifaceted—introducing groundbreaking innovation while raising questions about privacy and personal space. This chapter explores the intricate ways in which Generative AI influences our online interactions, focusing on its impact on social media. In the confluence of personal engagement and public conversation, Generative AI plays a pivotal role, crafting deeply personalized experiences that are universally accessible.

HOW GENERATIVE AI INFLUENCES YOUR SOCIAL MEDIA

Personalized Content Feeds

Imagine logging into your social media platform and finding relevant and engaging content that seems tailor-made for you. This is not a coincidence, but the work of Generative AI curates personalized content feeds by analyzing your interaction patterns, likes, shares, and even the amount of time you spend on specific posts. Through sophisticated algorithms, AI identifies your preferences and interests, dynamically adjusting the content it displays to keep you engaged and active on the platform. For instance, if you frequently interact with posts about renewable energy, AI ensures that similar content appears more prominently in your feed, creating an echo chamber of related information that resonates with your interests. This personalized experience saves you time and ensures you are always up to date with the topics that matter to you, making your social media experience more convenient and enjoyable.

This personalization extends beyond simple content delivery; it involves complex pattern recognition and predictive analytics, where

AI responds to your past behaviors and anticipates future interests based on broader trends and evolving preferences. Such capabilities make social media platforms adept at maintaining user engagement, but they also raise significant questions about the influence of AI-curated content on public discourse and individual choice.

AI in Content Creation

Generative AI also plays a pivotal role in content creation on social media, assisting in generating promotional content and personal posts that are likely to engage audiences. Brands and influencers leverage AI tools to create compelling images, videos, and text that resonate with their target demographics. These tools analyze vast amounts of engagement data to determine the elements that perform best—the text's tone, the colors in images, or the timing of posts.

For personal social media use, AI-driven applications can help craft posts that are optimized for engagement. For example, AI-powered photo-editing apps can enhance your photos to have maximum impact, applying filters or adjustments currently trending or preferred by your friends and followers. Generative AI can also suggest edits or enhancements to your posts, predicting what changes might increase likes, shares, and comments based on extensive data analysis. This way, you control the content you create, and AI is just a tool that helps you make it more engaging and appealing to your audience.

Enhancing User Interactions

Generative AI doesn't just curate content; it also enriches your interactions, adding depth and continuity to your conversations. By analyzing conversational data, AI can suggest contextually appropriate responses likely to foster further interaction. For example, if you're discussing a holiday, AI might suggest responses that ask about the destination or provide links to related content like travel deals or blogs, enhancing your conversation and making it more engaging.

AI's ability to facilitate richer interactions is grounded in its ability to understand and predict human communication patterns. By doing so, AI enhances user experience and fosters a sense of connection and community among users. However, as AI becomes more adept at shaping these interactions, the line between genuine human interaction and AI-mediated communication blurs, presenting new challenges for understanding and valuing our online engagements. These blurred lines can lead to losing authenticity and transparency in our online interactions, which are vital for building trust and maintaining healthy social relationships.

Ethical Considerations

The pervasive role of Generative AI in social media inevitably comes with a host of ethical considerations, particularly concerning privacy and data use. The data that AI uses to personalize content and enhance interactions is often profoundly personal, encompassing everything from our location and demographics to our private conversations and behavioral quirks. The handling, storage, and analysis of this data by AI systems pose significant privacy risks, making it imperative for users and platforms to ensure that data is used responsibly and transparently.

However, AI's potential to manipulate user behavior through personalized content raises ethical issues about autonomy and consent. Users must understand how their data shapes their online experiences and the extent to which AI influences their social interactions and information consumption. Striking a balance between personalization and privacy is challenging for AI in social media.

As we delve deeper into the capabilities and impacts of Generative AI across various sectors, understanding its role in shaping our online interactions is crucial. While these technologies enhance user experience and engagement, they also require careful consideration of ethical standards to ensure they contribute positively to our digital lives. We encourage you to continue exploring this topic and share your thoughts and questions.

ENHANCING ONLINE SHOPPING WITH GENERATIVE AI

In the bustling digital marketplace, where the convenience of online shopping meets the overwhelming abundance of product choices, Generative AI emerges as a pivotal ally, refining the shopping experience to cater to your unique preferences and needs. As you navigate online stores, AI quietly works in the background, analyzing your browsing behavior, past purchases, and even cursor movements to create a highly personalized shopping experience. This process involves sophisticated algorithms that understand your immediate needs and predict what products might interest you in the future. This personalized shopping experience saves you time and effort. It ensures that you find the products that best suit your needs, making your online shopping experience more satisfying, enjoyable, and, most importantly, secure.

Personalized Recommendations

The magic of personalized recommendations lies in Generative AI's ability to sift through enormous datasets to find patterns that take time to notice. For instance, if you have recently browsed outdoor camping gear, AI might recommend related items such as hiking boots or travel guides for national parks. These recommendations are dynamically tailored, changing as your browsing habits evolve. What makes this feature particularly powerful is its ability to learn from aggregate data across many users with similar interests, enhance its suggestions based on your actions, and incorporate insights from the preferences of others searching for or purchasing similar items. This method ensures that the recommendations are continuously refined, helping you discover products that perfectly match your preferences and, sometimes, pleasantly surprise you. This personalized shopping experience saves you time and effort and ensures you find the products that best suit your needs, making your online shopping experience more satisfying and enjoyable.

The implications of such personalized shopping experiences are profound. They significantly enhance user satisfaction by reducing the time spent searching for the right product. Additionally, they increase the likelihood of purchases, benefiting consumers and retailers. The sophistication of these recommendation systems continues to evolve, incorporating more nuanced data such as seasonal trends, regional popularity, and even current events to make predictions even more accurate and timely.

Visual Search Capabilities

Generative AI is also revolutionizing how you search for products online through visual search capabilities. Visual search allows you to load an image of an item, and AI will analyze it and return similar or complementary products available for purchase. For example, if you upload a picture of a floral dress you like, the AI can find similar dresses available in online stores or even suggest accessories that would match the dress. This technology works by analyzing the visual attributes of the image—colors, shapes, patterns—and comparing them with a vast database of product images to find matches.

This capability simplifies the search process and makes it more engaging, allowing for a more intuitive shopping experience that mimics how you might shop in a physical store. It is advantageous in industries where visual characteristics are paramount, such as fashion, home decor, and art. As visual search technology becomes more advanced, it can profoundly change online shopping, making it more interactive and responsive to your aesthetic preferences.

Dynamic Pricing Optimization

Dynamic pricing optimization is another critical area where Generative AI is significantly impacting. AI algorithms analyze various factors, including demand, inventory levels, competitor pricing, and user behavior, to adjust prices in real-time. This means that the price you see for a product may change based on when you look at it, how many people are viewing it, and how quickly it is selling. For retailers, this ability to adjust prices dynamically allows for better inventory management and profitability. For you, as a consumer, it means that you can find better deals if you purchase at the right time.

The complexity of dynamic pricing models lies in their need to balance profitability with customer satisfaction. If not managed carefully, high price fluctuation can lead to customer distrust or dissatisfaction. Therefore, AI systems are designed to ensure price changes are within acceptable limits, maintaining transparency with consumers about how prices are determined.

Customer Service Evolution

Finally, the evolution of customer service through AI chatbots and virtual assistants represents a significant shift in how post-purchase interactions are managed. AI-driven customer service solutions can handle many queries simultaneously, providing instant responses that help resolve issues or guide you through the purchase process.

These systems learn from each interaction, continuously improving their ability to resolve more complex queries.

Moreover, AI chatbots can personalize interactions based on your purchase history and preferences, sometimes even anticipating issues you might encounter. For instance, if a chatbot knows you have purchased a complex electronic device, it might proactively offer a setup guide or troubleshooting assistance. This proactive approach enhances your satisfaction and reduces the burden on human customer service representatives, allowing the customer service representative to focus on issues that require human intervention.

In online retail, the invisible hand of Generative AI is there, enhancing every step of your experience. From the moment you search for a product to the post-purchase support you may need, AI technologies transform online shopping into a highly personalized, efficient, and satisfying experience. As these technologies evolve, they promise further to blur the lines between digital convenience and customized service, offering a glimpse into the future of retail, where every shopping experience is as unique as the shopper.

CUSTOMIZING NEWS FEEDS AND ENTERTAINMENT

Generative AI is pivotal in customizing and enhancing how you engage with news and entertainment in digital media consumption. This technology leverages sophisticated algorithms to tailor content to your interests, transforming how you discover and interact with information and media. AI systems can construct highly personalized news feeds and entertainment suggestions by analyzing your previous interactions, viewing habits, and even the time you spend on specific types of content. This personalization extends beyond mere convenience; it fundamentally changes how you are informed and entertained, making your digital experiences more engaging and relevant to your tastes and preferences.

Generative AI is practical in content curation. AI algorithms continuously sift through vast content to recommend news articles, videos, podcasts, and more that align with your established interests. If you frequently read technology news, AI curates more articles about emerging tech and adapts to include related topics like tech policy or innovation in sectors you care about, like healthcare or education. This tailored approach ensures that your content is consistent with your interests and broadens your understanding of relevant subjects.

The impact of AI on the discovery of new content is profound. By analyzing patterns in your consumption behavior, AI can introduce you to new topics and media you might have yet to explore. This capability of AI to broaden your horizons is crucial in an age where the sheer volume of available content can seem overwhelming. For instance, if you are interested in classical music, AI might suggest a series on the evolution of classical music in cinema, connecting your interest with a new but related topic. This enriches your cultural and informational intake and enhances your engagement with the content, connecting different areas of interest in novel and meaningful ways.

Moreover, AI systems are designed to adapt to your feedback, continually refining their recommendations to improve accuracy and relevance. Your interaction with the curated content—whether you like, share, or spend time reading it—informs the AI about your preferences. This feedback loop allows AI to evolve its understanding of what engages you, fine-tuning its suggested content. Over time, this process enhances the AI's ability to predict what will keep you informed and entertained, ensuring a consistently engaging experience each time you log on. This adaptability is critical to maintaining a dynamic and responsive media consumption environment that resonates with your evolving interests and needs.

However, deploying AI to customize news feeds and entertainment is full of challenges. One significant concern is the creation of echo chambers, where the content you are exposed to increasingly reflects your existing beliefs and interests, potentially limiting your exposure to diverse perspectives and critical thinking. This phenomenon can have profound implications, particularly in how you perceive and understand world events, societal issues, and differing viewpoints. It is crucial, therefore, for AI systems to be designed with algorithms that not only personalize but also introduce diversity in the content they curate.

Privacy concerns also loom as AI systems require access to personal data to customize content effectively. Data collection, storage, and analysis, such as viewing history, interaction times, and content preferences, must be handled with stringent security measures and transparent privacy policies to protect you from potential data breaches and misuse. Ensuring you have control over your data and understand how it is used is essential for maintaining trust in the digital platforms that use AI to enhance your media consumption experience.

As Generative AI continues refining the digital news and entertainment arena, its potential to personalize and enhance media consumption holds promise and challenges. Navigating these will require careful consideration of ethical standards, privacy protections, and the design of AI systems that promote both personalization and exposure to a broad spectrum of content. As these technologies evolve, they will continue transforming how you discover, interact with, and enjoy digital content, aligning your online experiences with your preferences and continually adapting to your feedback.

Smart Homes and IoT: The Invisible Hand of Generative AI

In modern living, integrating Generative AI with Internet of Things ("IoT") devices is quietly revolutionizing our home environments, making them more intuitive, efficient, and attuned to our needs. Imagine living in a home where devices anticipate your preferences, manage your energy usage intelligently, and maintain themselves with minimal input from you. This concept is fast becoming a reality thanks to the sophisticated neural networks that power these smart devices.

Neural networks, particularly those designed for predictive maintenance and anomaly detection, are increasingly employed in IoT devices throughout our homes. These networks analyze continuous data streams from sensors embedded in devices like heating, ventilation, and air conditioning ("HVAC") systems, refrigerators, and washing machines. By processing this data, neural networks can detect patterns or anomalies that may indicate a potential malfunction. For example, a neural network might analyze the vibration patterns from a washing machine; a sudden change in the pattern could suggest a mechanical issue, prompting the system to alert you before the machine breaks down. The specific algorithms, such as convolutional neural networks ("CNNs") or recurrent neural networks ("RNNs"), are chosen based on their efficiency in processing time-series data or their ability to handle data with spatial hierarchies, making them ideal for predictive analysis.

The automation of home environments facilitated by Generative AI extends beyond maintenance. These AI systems integrate with home IoT devices to create living spaces that adapt to your life's rhythms, enhancing comfort, security, and efficiency. For instance, AI can learn your daily routine, automatically adjust the heating and lighting, and even play music to your taste, creating an atmosphere welcoming you as you arrive home. Security systems powered by AI enhance safety by distinguishing between regular activity and potential threats, like unknown visitors, and can alert you instantly through intelligent notifications.

Predictive maintenance, a crucial feature facilitated by Generative AI, ensures that smart home devices operate reliably. This AI capability involves continuous monitoring and analysis of the device's operation, predicting failures before they occur. By doing so, not only does it save the cost and hassle of unexpected repairs, but it also extends the lifespan of home appliances. For instance, an AI system might detect that the efficiency of your home's HVAC system is declining and suggest maintenance check-ups or filter changes that can preempt more severe issues.

Energy efficiency is another significant benefit of Generative AI in smart homes. These systems optimize energy use by learning and adapting to your living habits. For example, AI can control smart thermostats to reduce heating or cooling when you're not home or adjust the settings based on weather forecasts. Advanced AI algorithms can even participate in intelligent grids, managing energy consumption in response to peak load demands from the power grid, reducing costs, and contributing to energy sustainability.

Looking toward the future of smart living, the possibilities are expansive. Generative AI is set to drive innovations that could make homes reactive to our commands and proactive in managing our needs. We can anticipate developments where AI not only automates individual tasks but coordinates entire systems of devices to optimize our living conditions continuously. The societal impacts of such advancements could be profound, offering unprecedented efficiency and personalization in how we live. However, as we edge closer to these possibilities, considerations around data privacy, security, and the ethical use of AI remain paramount to ensure that these innovations align with societal values and contribute positively to our quality of life.

As we conclude this exploration of Generative AI in smart homes and IoT, it's clear that the technology is not just an added luxury but a transformative force in making our living spaces more responsive and sustainable. The seamless integration of AI with IoT devices represents a significant leap towards more connected, intelligent homes that understand and adapt to our needs. This chapter has unpacked how neural networks drive these innovations, the benefits of automating home environments, and the potential future advances in intelligent living. As we transition to the next chapter, we will explore how Generative AI is reshaping other facets of our daily lives, further highlighting its pervasive influence and the broad spectrum of its applications.

4. GENERATIVE AI FOR PERSONAL PRODUCTIVITY

Generative AI can boost worker productivity by as much as 40% compared with workers who don't use it.[1]

— MIT SLOAN

In the bustling corridors of modern workplaces, where the demands for efficiency and innovation are ever-increasing, Generative AI emerges as a revolutionary ally. Imagine a world where routine tasks are handled not by weary employees but by intelligent systems capable of learning and adapting. This chapter explores how Generative AI redefines productivity, allowing you to focus on what truly matters—creative and strategic thinking. Here, we'll see how embracing AI tools in your daily workflow can transform mundane tasks into opportunities for growth and innovation.

---

1. https://mitsloan.mit.edu/ideas-made-to-matter/how-generative-ai-can-boost-highly-skilled-workers-productivity

AUTOMATING ROUTINE TASKS WITH AI TOOLS

Streamlining Workflows

Generative AI is adept at automating routine administrative tasks that often consume a disproportionate amount of your workday. By taking over these tasks, AI allows you to allocate your time and mental energy towards more complex projects that require human creativity and strategic insight. For instance, AI can automate data entry and scheduling, two tasks that typically require meticulous attention to detail but little in the way of strategic thought. Imagine an AI system that not only schedules meetings based on everyone's availability but also sends out reminders and prepares agenda items by collating information from previous communications. Such systems are already transforming workplace dynamics by reducing administrative overhead and minimizing human error, thereby enhancing overall productivity.

Email and Communication

Communication is a cornerstone of effective business operations, yet managing emails and other communications can be overwhelmingly time-consuming. AI-driven tools are transforming this arena by helping you manage your inbox more efficiently. These tools use NLP to analyze your emails and prioritize them based on urgency and relevance. They can also suggest responses or automatically handle routine inquiries without your intervention. For example, an AI email assistant could draft preliminary responses to common questions like appointment requests or information queries, which you can review and personalize if necessary. This speeds up your response time and ensures you can focus on emails requiring direct and personal attention.

Enhancing Productivity

The transformative effect of Generative AI on workplace productivity cannot be overstated. When organizations adeptly incorporate AI-driven tools into their workflows, the results are a marked increase in employee satisfaction and operational efficiency. The reason behind this uptick in satisfaction is straightforward: AI shoulders the burden of monotonous, repetitive tasks. This shift enables employees to allocate more time and energy to engaging in meaningful and intellectually stimulating work. The ripple effect of this change is substantial, fostering a work environment where employees feel more valued and motivated. This heightened sense of job satisfaction is crucial, as it directly correlates with increased employee retention rates, effectively reducing the turnover that can disrupt and cost organizations considerably.

Furthermore, the intelligence that AI brings to the table accelerates the decision-making process. AI-driven tools analyze data and offer speed and accuracy insights that exceed human capabilities. This efficiency in generating insights means teams can arrive at well-informed decisions more swiftly, consequently cutting down the hours spent in deliberative meetings. The saved time can be redirected towards productive work, enhancing the organization's output. This compendium of improvements—from employee satisfaction to the streamlining of decision-making processes—culminates in developing an organizational culture that is more agile, responsive, and significantly more productive. Such a culture is well-equipped to adapt to changes and embrace innovation, ensuring the organization remains competitive and forward-thinking. Integrating Generative AI into the workplace is not merely about automating tasks; it's about reimagining the work environment to prioritize creativity, strategic engagement, and efficiency.

Data Analysis and Reporting

One of the most impactful applications of Generative AI is in data analysis and reporting. AI tools can analyze large datasets quickly and accurately, identifying trends and patterns that might go unnoticed by human analysts. These tools can generate comprehensive reports providing actionable strategic planning and decision-making insights. For instance, AI can track performance metrics across different company departments and generate visual reports highlighting areas of concern or opportunity. This capability not only makes data-driven decision-making accessible to non-experts but also ensures that such decisions are based on comprehensive and accurate data.

Enhancing Organizational Tools

Generative AI also significantly enhances the functionality of project management and organizational tools. By integrating AI, these tools can predict project timelines, allocate resources more efficiently, and identify potential bottlenecks before they cause delays. AI can also facilitate better collaboration among team members by suggesting task assignments based on individuals' skills and current workloads. For example, an AI-enhanced project management tool might notice a team member has a lower workload and automatically suggest reassigning some tasks to balance the team's workload more evenly.

Use Cases in Different Industries

The versatility of Generative AI in enhancing productivity is evident across various industries. AI tools automate risk assessment and fraud detection in finance, allowing analysts to focus on more complex financial strategies. AI streamlines administrative tasks such as appointment scheduling and patient data management in healthcare, enabling medical staff to prioritize patient care. In the arts, AI assists in managing logistical aspects of productions, such as budget tracking and resource allocation, freeing creative professionals to focus on the artistic components of their projects.

Challenges and Solutions

Despite its benefits, implementing AI solutions takes a lot of work. Resistance to change in workplace culture can hinder AI integration. Additionally, the initial setup and training of AI systems require time and resources. To overcome these challenges, it is essential to have a clear implementation strategy that includes training programs for employees, demonstrating the tangible benefits of AI tools. Moreover, choosing AI solutions that are user-friendly and well-supported by vendors can facilitate smoother transitions and encourage broader acceptance within the organization.

By using Generative AI, you can transform your approach to work, turning routine tasks into opportunities for innovation and strategic engagement. As AI evolves, its role in enhancing personal productivity will only increase, promising a future where our work lives are more creative and less consumed by the mundane.

USING GENERATIVE AI FOR LEARNING AND DEVELOPMENT

In education and professional development, integrating Generative AI into learning systems transforms how knowledge is acquired. These AI-driven systems employ sophisticated neural networks to analyze and adapt to individual learning patterns, providing a customized educational experience tailored to each learner's needs and pace. This personalization is achieved through continuous data analysis, where AI systems monitor the learner's interactions and progress, adjusting the content and teaching methods in real time to optimize learning outcomes.

AI in Adaptive Learning Systems

Neural networks, the backbone of these adaptive learning systems, meticulously process and learn from each learner's interaction with the content. For instance, if a learner struggles with a particular concept, the AI recognizes this through repeated incorrect answers or prolonged hesitations. It then adjusts the difficulty level of the subsequent content or revisits the troubling topic using different approaches or explanations. This adaptability enhances learning efficiency and keeps the learner engaged, as the content remains challenging yet achievable. Technical examples of such systems include platforms like DreamBoxLearning, which uses intelligent adaptive learning technology to provide mathematics education.

Here, the AI continuously assesses the student's answers and strategies, dynamically adjusting the curriculum to the student's learning speed and style.

Personalized Learning Paths

The power of Generative AI to customize learning experiences extends to creating personalized learning paths. By analyzing a learner's past performance, preferences, and even future career aspirations, AI systems can map out a unique educational adventure for everyone. This might involve suggesting specific courses that address skill gaps or recommending advanced studies in areas where the learner shows strong potential. Such personalized paths are particularly beneficial in higher education and professional development, where the focus is often on acquiring skills that align with career goals or market demands.

Content Generation

The capability of Generative AI to generate educational content is revolutionizing the way learning materials are created and distributed. AI can produce many learning aids, from quizzes and flashcards to interactive simulations and summaries, all tailored to the curriculum and the learner's progress. These materials supplement the learning experience and provide varied ways to engage with the content, catering to different learning styles. For example, an AI system might generate visual aids or interactive elements for visual learners while providing detailed textual explanations for those who prefer reading.

Language Learning

The impact of Generative AI in language learning is particularly notable. Language learning apps like Duolingo use AI to personalize lessons and practice sessions. The AI analyzes the learner's progress, focusing on areas that need improvement and adapting the difficulty level of exercises accordingly. It can also simulate natural conversation, providing learners valuable practice using the language in real-life scenarios. This personalized, interactive approach helps in faster and more effective language acquisition, making learning a new language more accessible to people worldwide.

Skill Acquisition and Enhancement

Generative AI is also crucial in skill acquisition and enhancement, especially in rapidly evolving fields such as technology and data science. AI-driven platforms can keep track of the latest developments and integrate them into the learning modules, ensuring that the learners are always up-to-date with current knowledge and practices. Additionally, AI can identify emerging trends and skills demanded by the market, guiding learners to acquire these competencies. For instance, an AI system might analyze job market trends and recommend a professional in marketing to learn data analytics, enhancing their skill set in line with market needs.

While using Generative AI in learning and development is immense, challenges such as ensuring the quality and accuracy of AI-generated content and maintaining an up-to-date curriculum encompassing the latest industry trends are ongoing. Overcoming these challenges involves continuously monitoring and updating AI algorithms and curricula and collaborating with educators, developers, and industry experts to ensure that educational content meets quality standards and remains relevant and practical.

As we continue to explore the abilities of Generative AI in transforming education, it becomes clear that these technologies offer unprecedented opportunities for personalized, efficient, and dynamic learning experiences. By adapting to personal learning styles and needs, AI empowers learners to achieve their full potential, making education more accessible and effective for everyone.

CREATIVE WRITING AND ART MAKING WITH AI

In the vibrant intersection of technology and creativity, Generative AI is not just a tool but a collaborator, enhancing the artistic and literary processes by providing a wellspring of ideas, themes, and styles. For artists and writers, confronting a blank canvas or an empty page can be daunting. Generative AI intervenes here as a muse, offering a cascade of suggestions that can spark creativity. These AI tools access a vast database of artistic and literary works, analyzing patterns, styles, and themes to propose original concepts. For example, an AI might suggest a narrative theme based on trending social issues or a painting style that combines elements from different art movements, thereby providing a fresh perspective that can ignite the creative process.

This stimulation is particularly valuable when you find yourself grappling with creative blocks. AI's ability to generate prompts, sketches, or drafts based on your initial inputs can serve as a creative lifeline, transforming vague ideas into tangible starting points. If a writer inputs a basic plot outline, the AI can suggest several plot twists or character developments, each branching into different narrative directions. For an artist, entering a mood or a preferred color palette can lead the AI to generate preliminary sketches that capture the desired emotion or tone. These aids are not just about providing answers but about opening new doors for creative exploration, making the creative experience less isolating and more dynamic.

The collaborative nature of human-AI art creation is transforming traditional artistic workflows. AI is a co-creator in this partnership, bringing its vast computational capacity to bear on creative challenges. This collaboration is evident in projects where poets use AI to craft verses refined by human creativity or in digital art installations where AI algorithms generate evolving visual elements that respond to audience interactions. The result is a new form of art that is interactive, ever-changing, and reflective of a blend of human emotion and AI capabilities. This synergy expands the boundaries of what can be achieved creatively and democratizes artmaking, allowing individuals without formal training to express their creativity supported by AI.

However, integrating AI into creative domains raises significant ethical and copyright considerations that must be meticulously navigated. One of the primary concerns is the originality and ownership of AI-generated work. Who holds the copyright if AI predominantly creates a piece of literature or artwork? Is it the creator of the AI, the user who provided the initial input, or the AI itself? These questions are not merely academic; they have practical implications for valuing and monetizing creative works. Furthermore, there's the ethical dilemma of authenticity and expression in art. Can a work be considered art if the emotional and experiential inputs typically associated with creative expression are absent or generated by algorithms?

These pressing questions provoke a broader discussion about the role of AI in creative fields. They challenge us to reconsider our definitions of creativity and authorship in the age of artificial intelligence. As Generative AI continues to evolve, it will be crucial for artists, writers, and policymakers to engage in ongoing dialogues about these issues to ensure that AI enhances human creativity without undermining the value of human artistic expression.

For those eager to explore AI-generated art and writing further, there are numerous online platforms where you can interact with AI art generators and text creators. These platforms allow you to input your ideas and see how AI transforms them into unique artworks or narratives. Engaging with these tools can help you understand the capabilities and limitations of Generative AI in creative processes and inspire you to integrate AI into your artistic or literary projects. Here, you can scan

to access an AI art generator that allows you to create digital paintings based on your inputs about mood, style, and color preferences, offering a hands-on experience of AI as a co-creator in the artistic process.

PLANNING YOUR TRAVEL WITH GENERATIVE AI ASSISTANCE

In an era where travel complexity often overshadows the joy of exploration, Generative AI emerges meticulously crafting travel experiences tailored to your tastes, budget constraints, and time availability. This technology's ability to distill vast amounts of travel data into coherent, actionable travel plans marks a significant evolution in how we plan and experience our adventures. Imagine a system that understands your preference for boutique hotels, your fascination with culinary adventures, or your need for relaxation and crafts a travel itinerary that feels personally curated just for you. Generative AI takes personalized travel to another level.

Generative AI excels in creating these customized travel plans by leveraging sophisticated algorithms that analyze your past travel experiences, reviews you've interacted with, and your saved or liked destinations on travel platforms. By integrating this information with real-time data such as weather forecasts, local events, and seasonal tourist trends, AI can propose travel itineraries that match your personal preferences and consider external factors that could influence your trip. For instance, if you enjoy quiet, scenic vacations, AI might suggest a lesser-known coastal town over a bustling beach resort, mainly if real-time data indicates that popular spots are currently overcrowded or under weather advisories. The efficiency and customization AI provides make travel planning more straightforward and exciting, as each itinerary uniquely suits your travel narrative.

Moreover, the power of AI extends to providing detailed recommendations on destinations, accommodations, and activities. By analyzing extensive databases containing millions of traveler reviews, photos, and descriptions, AI algorithms identify patterns and preferences unique to your travel style. These systems can suggest destinations that align with your interests, such as cultural hubs for art lovers or adventure camps for thrill-seekers. Accommodations are also offered based on your preferred style of travel; luxury seekers are directed towards highly rated boutique hotels, while budget-conscious travelers are shown comfortable but cost-effective options. Activities are suggested by analyzing what others with similar tastes have enjoyed, ensuring your travel experience is personalized and enriching.

The logistical aspect of travel, often the most tedious, is significantly streamlined by AI tools. These systems compare travel options, from flights to train tickets, to find the best cost, convenience, and comfort. AI algorithms are particularly adept at predicting price trends based on historical information and current market dynamics, advising you on the optimal times to book flights or hotels. This capability simplifies the booking process and ensures you get the most value for your money, potentially saving you from the price hikes affecting less informed travelers.

Enhancing your travel experience further, AI plays a crucial role during the trip itself by providing real-time assistance and cultural insights. This on-trip assistance is facilitated through mobile apps integrated with AI, which offer guidance and information at your fingertips. Whether it's navigating local transport, finding the best nearby dining options that meet your dietary preferences, or offering insights into local customs and language tips, AI makes traveling in unfamiliar territories less daunting and more enriching. These apps often include features that adapt to your location and activities, providing context-specific recommendations and alerts that enhance your safety and enjoyment.

As Generative AI continues to evolve, its integration into travel planning and management represents a profound shift towards more personalized, efficient, and enjoyable travel experiences. By handling everything from the macro elements of itinerary planning to the micro-details of day-to-day activities, AI not only enhances the logistical aspects of travel but also enriches the experiential aspects, allowing you to immerse fully in the joys of discovery without the traditional burdens of travel planning. This shift is not merely about technological advancement but redefining how we experience the world. As such, Generative AI stands as a cornerstone of modern travel, turning the chaos of planning into the art of experiencing, ensuring that each adventure you undertake is as unique as you are.

PERSONAL FINANCE AND BUDGETING WITH AI

In the intricate world of personal finance, where keeping track of expenses and optimizing investments can often seem daunting, Generative AI is emerging as a transformative tool. This technology simplifies the complex, making understanding and managing your financial health easier. Imagine a system that tracks every penny you spend and provides tailored advice on budgeting those pennies better. Generative AI does precisely this by integrating sophisticated algorithms that analyze your financial data in real time, offering insights that are not just data-rich but also incredibly actionable.

Automated Expense Tracking and Analysis

The first step towards adequate personal finance is understanding where your money goes. Generative AI excels in this area by automatically tracking and categorizing your expenses. Through direct links to your financial accounts, AI systems can pull in data from bank transactions, credit cards, and even cash purchases entered manually. These systems use machine learning to categorize each expense into buckets such as utilities, groceries, or entertainment, allowing you to see a clear picture of your spending patterns. More sophisticated AI can even identify anomalies or unusual spending behaviors, alerting you to potential fraud or areas where you might overspend without realizing it. This detailed, automated tracking level helps illuminate your financial scenario, making managing and controlling your spending more manageable.

Personalized Budgeting Advice

Beyond tracking, Generative AI provides personalized budgeting advice tailored to your financial goals and habits. By analyzing your income, recurring expenses, and saving goals, AI can create a customized budget plan that suggests how much you should ideally spend per category. If you aim to save for a down payment on a house, the AI might suggest adjustments in discretionary spending areas, like dining out or shopping, to help you meet your target faster. This personalized advice considers your current financial situation and future goals, providing a holistic approach to budget management that is both supportive and practical.

Investment and Savings Optimization

Generative AI acts as a savvy financial advisor for growing your wealth. Using historical data, market trends, and predictive analytics, AI can suggest investment strategies aligning with your risk tolerance and economic objectives. Whether recommending a diverse portfolio of stocks and bonds or suggesting the right time to invest in market opportunities, AI provides insights informed by a vast array of data points that would be difficult for individual investors to analyze. Furthermore, AI can monitor savings accounts and recommend when to shift funds into higher-yielding accounts or investment opportunities, ensuring your money is safe and growing.

Predicting Financial Health

One of the most forward-thinking applications of Generative AI in personal finance is its ability to predict your future financial health. AI can forecast your financial trajectory by analyzing current spending, saving patterns, and external economic factors. This forecast can help you understand future financial challenges and opportunities, allowing you to make data-driven decisions that safeguard your financial stability. For instance, if the AI predicts a potential cash flow issue based on upcoming expenses and current savings, it can advise you to adjust your spending or explore additional income sources. This predictive capability is invaluable, providing a forward-looking approach to financial planning that helps you stay one step ahead.

Through these applications, Generative AI simplifies personal finance and empowers you to take proactive steps toward achieving your financial goals. It transforms data into insights, expenses into opportunities for savings, and financial planning into a dynamic, interactive process that supports your financial well-being.

As we close this chapter on the transformative impact of Generative AI on personal finance, we are reminded of the broader potential of AI to enhance our daily lives. AI's vast and varied capabilities, from automating mundane tasks to personalizing learning and revolution-izing financial management. This exploration highlights practical applications and underscores the importance of integrating AI into our personal and professional spheres to harness its full potential. As we turn to the next chapter, we will probe the ethical dimensions of AI, a critical consideration as we seek to investigate the use of AI in business and industry.

5. Generative AI in Business and Industry

Generative AI is the next great frontier for businesses, transforming how we interact with customers and tailor experiences at an individual level.[1]

— Bernard Marr

Imagine walking into a store where the displays, products, and promotions perfectly align with your tastes and preferences, almost as if the store knows you personally. This scenario is rapidly becoming a reality as businesses leverage Generative AI to transform marketing and customer engagement. In this chapter, we will explore how Generative AI enhances and revolutionizes business operations, offering unprecedented precision and efficiency in understanding and catering to customers.

---

1. Marr, B. (2021). *The Intelligence Revolution: Transforming Your Business With AI*, Wiley.

REVOLUTIONIZING MARKETING WITH GENERATIVE AI

In the fast-evolving domain of marketing, Generative AI acts as a catalyst for creativity and insight, providing businesses with the tools to craft marketing strategies that are not only effective but also highly personalized and engaging.

Automated Content Creation

Generative AI facilitates rapidly producing marketing materials that resonate deeply with diverse audiences. By leveraging data-driven insights, these AI systems can generate content, from email campaigns to social media posts, tailored to different market segments' tastes and preferences. For example, a Generative AI tool can analyze data from previous campaigns, extracting well-performing elements and using this information to craft new content replicating successful themes or messages while introducing novel ideas to maintain freshness and engagement. This capability speeds up content creation and enhances relevance, significantly boosting engagement rates.

Customer Insights and Personalization

The role of AI in extracting and analyzing customer data is paramount in personalizing marketing strategies. By understanding patterns in customer behavior, preferences, and feedback, AI systems can help businesses tailor product offerings to meet the personalized needs of their customers. For instance, an AI system may analyze purchasing information to identify which products are frequently bought together, enabling the company to make targeted recommendations to other customers with similar buying habits. This level of personalization improves customer satisfaction and increases the likelihood of repeat business.

Virtual Product Demonstrations

AI is transforming how products are showcased through virtual demonstrations that allow customers to experience products in a highly interactive and realistic manner. For example, AI-driven virtual reality setups can simulate the experience of using a product in different environments, helping customers make informed purchasing decisions. These demonstrations benefit furniture, where buyers can visualize how different pieces look in their homes. AI increases customer engagement and reduces the likelihood of returns since buyers have a more explicit expectation of the product.

Predictive Marketing Strategies

Generative AI excels in predicting future market trends and consumer behaviors, allowing companies to prepare and adapt their strategies proactively. By analyzing current market data and comparing it with historical trends, AI models can forecast future changes in consumer preferences, economic shifts, and even potential new markets. This predictive capability enables businesses to stay ahead of the curve, allocating resources more effectively and seizing opportunities before the competition.

Competitive Advantage

Businesses integrating Generative AI into marketing strategies gain a significant competitive edge, particularly in market analysis and customer insight. AI tools can process substantial amounts of data much more quickly and accurately than human analysts, providing companies with real-time insights that can be immediately leveraged to refine marketing strategies continuously. This rapid, data-driven approach helps companies respond more swiftly to market changes, aligning offerings with customer expectations and improving market share and profitability.

Ethical Use of Data

While the advantages of using Generative AI in marketing are considerable, it is imperative to approach these technologies with a solid ethical framework, particularly concerning the use of consumer data. Ensuring data privacy, securing informed consent for data collection, and maintaining transparency about how information is used are crucial. Businesses must adhere to these principles to comply with regulations and build and maintain customer trust. Ethical considerations should be at the forefront of any AI-driven strategy, ensuring technology enhances customer relationships rather than undermines them.

Interactive Element: Virtual Product Demo Experience

I have included an interactive virtual demo setup to give you a first-hand understanding of how AI-driven virtual product demonstrations enhance customer engagement. This setup allows you to experience a virtual home environment where you can interact with various home appliances, observing how they work and fit into different home settings. This exercise illustrates the practical application of AI in marketing and emphasizes the immersive potential of modern marketing techniques.

Generative AI transforms businesses' marketing strategies and sets new customer engagement and satisfaction standards. Combining technology and creativity in business leads to innovative marketing solutions that resonate deeply with consumers, fostering a data-driven and distinctly human connection.

ENHANCING CUSTOMER SERVICE WITH GENERATIVE AI

In today's fast-paced digital environment, customer service is more than just handling inquiries; it's about creating a customer experience that leaves customers feeling valued and understood. Generative AI is revolutionizing this space by integrating advanced AI-powered tools such as chatbots and virtual assistants, which provide round-the-clock customer service. These AI technologies can understand and process natural language, allowing them to interpret customer queries and respond in an informed and human-like manner. For instance, an AI chatbot in a banking service can not only answer questions about account balances or transaction histories. However, it can also assist in more complex requests, such as disputing transactions or setting up new accounts without human intervention. This capability ensures that customer service is immediate and practical, reducing wait times and improving customer satisfaction.

The integration of AI in customer service extends beyond mere interaction handling; it personalizes the customer experience, making each interaction more relevant and engaging. AI systems can tailor their responses to customer needs and preferences by analyzing past interactions and preferences. For example, if a customer frequently asks about specific product features, the AI can remember these preferences and highlight relevant product recommendations or promotions in future interactions. This personalization fosters a sense of loyalty and satisfaction among customers, as they receive service that feels bespoke and considerate, acknowledging their unique needs and history with the brand.

Furthermore, Generative AI significantly enhances the efficiency and scalability of customer service operations. Traditional customer service frameworks often need help to scale during peak times, leading to increased wait times and decreased customer satisfaction. AI systems, however, can handle thousands of interactions simultaneously without compromising the quality of service. This scalability ensures that customer inquiries are addressed promptly and allows businesses to manage resources more effectively. Instead of allocating a large workforce to manage customer interactions, companies can deploy AI solutions to handle routine inquiries and direct more complex issues to human agents. This strategy optimizes operational efficiency and allows human customer service representatives to focus on problems that require empathy and deep problem-solving skills, ultimately enhancing the overall quality of service.

The collaboration between AI and human agents in customer service is a delicate balance that can significantly enhance service delivery. While AI excels in handling routine tasks and managing extensive interactions, human agents bring empathy, understanding, and complex problem-solving skills crucial for specific customer interactions. For example, in handling a sensitive complaint or negotiating a service issue, human agents can understand nuances and provide compassion and assurance that AI might not fully replicate. By integrating AI to handle initial inquiries and routine tasks, businesses can ensure that human agents are more available for interactions that require a personal touch, thus optimizing the customer service process and ensuring that each customer receives the attention they need.

In integrating Generative AI into customer service, businesses enhance efficiency and craft more prosperous, personalized customer interactions. As AI technology continues to evolve, its role in transforming customer service remains a compelling narrative of innovation, personalization, and enhanced operational efficiency, ensuring that businesses can meet the high standards of service that customers expect in today's digital world.

INNOVATIONS IN HEALTHCARE: AI'S ROLE IN PERSONALIZED MEDICINE

In healthcare, Generative AI is proving to be a tool and a transformative force, particularly in personalized medicine. This technology's ability to integrate and analyze vast amounts of complex medical data is revolutionizing diagnostic processes. Traditionally, medical diagnostics have relied heavily on medical professionals' accumulated knowledge and experience. However, Generative AI introduces a new dimension to diagnostic accuracy and speed by leveraging patterns found in extensive datasets that no human could feasibly analyze. For instance, AI systems can now review thousands of radiographic images to detect subtle signs of diseases such as cancer at stages so early that they often go unnoticed by human eyes. Moreover, these systems can integrate diverse data types, including genetic information and patient medical histories, to enhance diagnostic precision. This capability increases accuracy, significantly speeds up diagnostic and intervention, and improves patient outcomes.

The impact of Generative AI extends beyond diagnostics into the customization of treatment plans. Each patient responds differently to treatments based on their unique genetic makeup, and here, AI's ability to tailor medical solutions shines brightly. By analyzing genetic data alongside existing medical records and ongoing research, AI systems can identify which remedies are likely to be most effective for individual patients. This approach is revolutionary in fields like oncology, where AI-driven analysis of a tumor's genetic mutations can help oncologists choose a cancer treatment tailored to the patient's specific condition. This personalized treatment increases the efficacy and minimizes the side effects and unnecessary medical costs associated with less targeted therapy approaches. The integration of AI in developing these customized treatment plans marks a significant shift towards more patient-centered, precision medicine.

Drug Discovery and Development

One of the most exciting applications of Generative AI in healthcare is drug discovery and development. Traditionally, the drug development process is time-consuming and very costly, often taking over a decade and billions of dollars to move from concept to market. Generative AI is poised to disrupt this process by significantly accelerating the pace of drug discovery. AI algorithms can quickly analyze molecular structures and biological datasets to identify potential drug candidates that human researchers might overlook. These AI systems can also predict how different chemical compounds will react with each other, allowing researchers to simulate drug trials and identify promising drug candidates much earlier in the development process. For example, AI-driven platforms are currently being used to develop drugs for diseases that are difficult to treat with traditional methods, such as certain types of cancer and neurological disorders.

Patient engagement and education are also being enhanced through Generative AI. Educating patients about their health conditions and requisite treatments is crucial for adequate healthcare. AI systems can now generate personalized educational content tailored to patients' needs and comprehension levels. For example, an AI system can generate interactive 3D models visually explaining a patient's disease process or treatment procedure. This model can be customized to the patient's medical imaging and data, providing a highly personalized educational tool. Moreover, AI-driven platforms can provide patients with ongoing support and learning opportunities, adapting content to reflect changes in their health conditions or treatment responses. This adaptive learning approach empowers patients with knowledge about their health and engages them more actively in their treatment processes, potentially leading to better health outcomes.

Challenges and Future Prospects

Despite its potential, applying Generative AI in science and healthcare is challenging. The complex biological systems and the variability in individual health conditions mean that AI systems must be incredibly sophisticated to be effective. Data quality is a significant concern, as AI systems require enormous amounts of high-quality data to learn effectively. Poor-quality data sets can lead to inaccurate predictions and potentially harmful outcomes, particularly in healthcare applications.

Technical challenges such as algorithmic stability and computational costs also pose significant barriers to the widespread adoption of Generative AI in these fields. Algorithmic stability refers to the ability of AI systems to provide consistent and reliable results even when faced with variable data inputs. Unstable algorithms can lead to inconsistent treatment recommendations, undermining trust in AI-driven systems. The high computational costs associated with training and running sophisticated AI models also limit the ability of many organizations to implement these technologies effectively.

Despite these challenges, the future of Generative AI in science and healthcare looks promising. Ongoing advancements in AI technology, including improvements in data quality and algorithmic stability, are making it possible to overcome many current limitations. As these technologies continue to evolve, they are expected to become more accessible and widely used, potentially transforming these fields in ways that are currently hard to imagine. Integrating Generative AI into scientific research and healthcare could significantly enhance our understanding and treatment of complex diseases, paving the way for a future where medical care is more effective, efficient, and personalized.

Generative AI in Content Creation: Blogs, Videos, and More

In the digital era, content is king. However, the throne is increasingly occupied by Generative AI, a transformative force reshaping content creation across blogs, videos, and graphics. This technology not only streamlines the production of content but significantly enhances the creative processes behind it, offering fresh perspectives and innovative ideas that captivate audiences.

Content Generation

Generative AI is a dynamic tool in the arsenal of content creators, assisting in generating written content, videos, and graphics. This technology utilizes advanced algorithms to analyze existing content and develop new pieces that are both original and relevant. For instance, in blogging, AI can suggest content themes based on trending topics or user engagement, draft initial article outlines, and write complete blog posts requiring minimal human editing. In video production, AI tools can script video sequences, generate synthesized voice-overs, and edit raw footage into polished final products. Similarly, in graphic design, AI-powered software can produce compelling visuals, including infographics and branding materials, that align with specific design principles and brand aesthetics. These capabilities expedite creation and ensure the content is optimized for maximum impact and engagement.

Enhancing Creativity

While some may fear that AI might stifle human creativity, the reality is quite the contrary. Generative AI is a collaborative partner that augments human creativity by generating new ideas and perspectives that might take time to become apparent. This partnership is particularly evident in brainstorming sessions where AI can offer novel concepts or alternative approaches, pushing human creators to explore new creative territories. Additionally, AI can handle the more mundane aspects of creative work, such as data gathering and initial drafts, allowing human creators to focus on the more nuanced and emotionally resonant elements of content creation. This synergy between human ingenuity and artificial intelligence opens new horizons in creative expression, enabling content that is not only innovative but also profoundly resonant with audiences.

SEO and Audience Engagement

In the competitive world of digital content, visibility is paramount. Here, Generative AI plays a crucial role by optimizing content for search engines and improving audience engagement. AI tools analyze critical metrics from previous content to identify patterns that drive user engagement and search engine rankings. Armed with this data, AI can guide the creation of new content better tailored to audience preferences and optimized for SEO. For instance, AI can recommend keywords, predict headline effectiveness, and suggest content structures more likely to engage readers and rank favorably on search engines. This targeted approach enhances content visibility and ensures it resonates with its intended audience, leading to higher engagement rates and more sustained interaction.

Ethical and Quality Considerations

As the use of Generative AI in content creation grows, so do the associated ethical considerations and quality concerns. One of the primary concerns is the authenticity and originality of AI-generated content. While AI can produce content that mimics human writing or artistic style, whether this content can be considered "original" or "authentic" remains a topic of debate. To address this, it is crucial to maintain transparency about AI's contribution to content creation, ensuring that audiences know the technology's role. Additionally, ethical guidelines should govern the use of AI in content creation, ensuring that it supports human creativity rather than replaces it.

Technical Limitations and Quality Assurance

Despite its advanced capabilities, Generative AI has limitations, particularly in areas prone to misinformation or subtle nuances of human communication. These limitations can affect the quality and authenticity of AI-generated content, potentially leading to inaccuracies or ethical issues. Integrating human oversight into creating AI content is essential to mitigate these risks. Human editors can review AI-generated content for accuracy, moral concerns, and alignment with the brand's voice, ensuring that the final product maintains high standards of quality and integrity. Additionally, continuous training of AI models on updated and verified data sets can help minimize errors and adapt AI outputs to changing norms and expectations.

GENERATIVE AI IN LOGISTICS

Generative AI is a transformative force in the intricate and fast-paced logistics business. It optimizes supply chain operations, enhances demand forecasting, and improves logistical efficiencies through sophisticated route optimization and autonomous vehicle navigation. Integrating AI into logistics is not just about automation but about creating smarter, more responsive systems that can instantly adapt to changing conditions and deliver efficiencies on a previously unattainable scale.

Introduction to AI in Logistics

Generative AI streamlines logistics operations by predicting and managing the complexities of supply chain dynamics. For instance, AI systems analyze historical data and current market trends to forecast product demand accurately. This predictive power allows companies to optimize inventory levels, reducing overstock and minimizing out-of-stock scenarios, which can lead to lost sales. Additionally, AI-driven route optimization algorithms process real-time traffic data, weather conditions, and vehicle performance metrics to optimize route efficiency for delivery vehicles. This cuts down delivery times and reduces fuel consumption and operational costs. In more advanced applications, autonomous cars equipped with AI navigate complex environments independently, further enhancing delivery efficiencies and reducing the need for human intervention.

Case Studies

Consider the implementation of AI in the logistics operations of global giants like Amazon and Alibaba. These companies utilize AI to manage vast warehouses where goods are sorted, packed, and shipped worldwide. At Amazon, AI-driven systems predict order volumes and guide inventory placement throughout the warehouse to minimize the time required to retrieve items during order fulfillment. Robots autonomously navigate the warehouse floors, picking and transporting items based on AI-generated routes that avoid collisions and reduce bottlenecks. Similarly, Alibaba's logistics arm, Cainiao, uses AI to optimize its global logistics network, predicting parcel volumes and delivery routes to ensure timely and cost-effective delivery.

Another illustrative case is Maersk, the world's largest container shipping company, which employs AI to enhance its operational efficiency. Maersk uses AI to predict transit times more accurately, helping customers plan their supply chains better. AI algorithms analyze historical shipping data and real-time weather reports to forecast potential delays, allowing the company to proactively manage its shipping schedules and maintain service reliability even under adverse conditions.

Challenges in AI-Driven Logistics

Despite these successes, scaling AI solutions from pilot projects to full-scale deployments across global supply chains presents significant challenges. Integrating AI into legacy logistics systems often involves substantial initial costs and can disrupt existing operations. Moreover, the complexity of global supply chains means that AI systems must be highly robust and adaptable to varying regulations, market conditions, and logistical challenges across different regions.

Data security is another critical issue, especially given the sensitive nature of the data involved in logistics operations, including customer information, supplier details, and real-time location data of shipments. Protecting this data against breaches is paramount, as any compromise could disrupt operations, damage a company's reputation, and lead to significant financial losses.

Future Outlook

Looking to the future, the possibilities for AI in logistics appear boundless. Fully autonomous logistics operations could become the norm, from self-managing warehouses to drone-based delivery systems. Integrating AI with the Internet of Things devices in logistics is also a promising area for development. IoT devices can collect real-time data from every corner of the supply chain. AI can analyze the data to provide insights that help optimize logistics operations, from warehouse management to last-mile delivery.

As Generative AI continues to evolve, its role in logistics is set to grow, potentially transforming the industry into a model of efficiency and precision. Adopting AI in logistics promises significant cost reductions and speed improvements and offers the agility needed to respond to an ever-changing global market. As companies navigate these opportunities and challenges, the future of logistics will increasingly be defined by the ability to integrate and leverage AI technologies effectively.

GENERATIVE AI IN REAL ESTATE

Generative AI in real estate is helpful because it can analyze complex market trends, generate virtual property tours, and predict maintenance needs with unprecedented accuracy. This technology enhances and redefines existing processes, offering both real estate professionals and clients a more efficient, personalized, and informed real estate experience.

AI-Driven Market Analysis

The application of Generative AI in real estate market analysis profoundly reshapes how agents, buyers, and sellers interact with the market. Using sophisticated machine learning models, Generative AI processes vast arrays of data, including historical price trends, community statistics, and economic indicators, to provide a nuanced analysis of current market conditions. This capability allows real estate professionals to offer clients more accurate, data-driven advice, from pricing their homes to choosing the right buying time. For example, by analyzing patterns in housing price fluctuations and correlating them with local economic shifts, AI can predict future market trends, helping clients make more informed investment decisions. This level of analysis was traditionally time-consuming and prone to human error, but AI now delivers rapid, precise assessments that significantly enhance decision-making processes.

Virtual Tours and Staging

Generative AI also revolutionizes how properties are showcased to potential buyers by creating virtual tours and digital staging. AI algorithms can generate realistic 3D models of properties, allowing prospective buyers to explore homes virtually without the need to visit in person. This technology is particularly beneficial in today's global market, where buyers may be anywhere. Additionally, AI-driven staging tools can furnish these virtual spaces with various decorative styles, helping buyers visualize themselves in the home. This makes the viewing process more convenient and engaging, as buyers can customize the home's appearance to suit their tastes, making it easier to connect emotionally with the property.

Predictive Maintenance

Beyond assisting in sales, Generative AI plays a vital role in property management through predictive maintenance. AI can predict when property elements may need repair or replacement by analyzing data from various sensors and systems within a building. This proactive approach to maintenance helps property managers and homeowners avoid the inconvenience and cost of unexpected breakdowns. For instance, AI might analyze data from a heating system, predict the likelihood of a malfunction, and suggest maintenance before the system fails, ensuring the property remains comfortable and functional for its occupants. This helps maintain the property value and enhances the satisfaction of tenants and owners alike.

Ethical Considerations

However, as with all AI applications, there are ethical considerations to address, particularly regarding the potential for bias in AI algorithms. In real estate, biased AI models could unfairly affect property valuations or loan approvals, disadvantaging certain groups based on demographics inferred from data such as zip codes or income levels. It is crucial, therefore, for developers and users of real estate AI tools to ensure that the data used to train these models is as unbiased as possible and to continually monitor and update these models to prevent discriminatory practices. Transparency in how AI models make decisions is also essential, as it fosters trust among all parties involved—buyers, sellers, and real estate professionals.

Generative AI in real estate will make the market more accessible, efficient, and fair. As these tools become more sophisticated and widespread, they offer the potential to transform every aspect of real estate, from the initial search for a property to the management and maintenance of real estate portfolios. While challenges remain, particularly in ensuring ethical application and preventing bias, the future of real estate looks increasingly digital, data-driven, and AI-enhanced, providing opportunities for innovation and improvement at every turn.

GENERATIVE AI IN ROBOTICS

The integration of Generative AI into the field of robotics marks a pivotal shift towards more autonomous and intelligent systems capable of performing a wide array of tasks, from intricate surgical procedures to everyday household chores. These advancements are primarily fueled by AI's ability to process and learn from vast datasets, simulate numerous scenarios, and generate real-time adaptive responses. The application of Generative AI in robotics allows these machines to perform predetermined tasks and adapt their actions based on changing environmental conditions or task requirements.

In manufacturing, healthcare, and service industries, the demands placed on robots vary significantly, necessitating a level of customization that traditional robotics could not quickly achieve. Generative AI facilitates this by enabling robots to learn from diverse data, including visual inputs, sensor readings, and human interactions, allowing them to handle tasks requiring high precision and adaptability. For instance, in manufacturing, robots equipped with AI can switch from assembling one type of product to another without extensive reprogramming. This adaptability is achieved through machine learning algorithms that enable the robot to learn from each task and improve its performance over time.

The role of AI in creating innovative robot designs also cannot be overstated. By utilizing advanced algorithms, robotics engineers can design machines that can perform complex tasks more efficiently and safely. For example, AI-driven simulations can help engineers test different robot designs in virtual environments to determine the most effective configurations before the actual manufacturing process begins. This saves time and resources and ensures that the robots are as safe as possible, reducing the risk of accidents in environments like factories and hospitals.

AI-powered robots transform manufacturing lines by enhancing speed, precision, and flexibility. These robots perform tasks such as welding, painting, and assembly with high precision, ensuring that products are manufactured to a very high standard. Additionally, AI enables these robots to quickly adapt to new manufacturing processes, which is crucial in industries where product designs frequently change. The ability of AI-powered robots to learn and adapt in real time reduces downtime and increases productivity, making manufacturing processes more efficient.

The healthcare industry benefits similarly from the precision and adaptability of AI-driven robotics. Robotic assistants in surgeries, for instance, use real-time data to make precise movements that enhance the surgeon's capabilities. These robots can adjust their actions in response to minute changes in the patient's condition or the surgeon's commands, improving the precision of surgical procedures and reducing the risk of complications. Furthermore, robots in healthcare settings perform repetitive tasks such as dispensing medication, allowing medical people to prioritize more critical aspects of patient care.

Service robots, deployed in public spaces and homes, are becoming increasingly common because of the evolution of Generative AI. In hospitality, robots personalize guest interactions, adjusting their responses based on guest preferences and behaviors. In elder care, robots assist with daily activities, adapting their support to the changing needs of individuals. As personal assistants, these robots manage schedules, control smart home devices, and provide timely reminders, enhancing the quality of life for their users.

However, integrating sophisticated AI systems into robotics is challenging. Compatibility issues often arise when integrating AI with existing robotic platforms, particularly in systems not originally designed to support advanced AI capabilities. Additionally, the hardware used in some older robots may not support the latest AI software, requiring significant modifications or complete overhauls of the robotic systems.

Reliability and safety concerns are also paramount, especially when robots interact closely with humans. The unpredictability of human environments means that robots must be highly reliable and safe to prevent accidents. Moreover, as robots become more autonomous, ensuring they perform tasks without causing harm becomes increasingly challenging.

Scalability remains another significant hurdle, particularly when customizing AI solutions for different types of robots and operational scales. Developing AI systems that can be efficiently scaled and adapted to various robotic platforms is crucial for the widespread integration of AI in robotics.

Ethical and societal considerations also play a critical role in deploying robots, especially those used in personal and public spaces. Privacy implications arise when robots with surveillance capabilities collect and store personal data. Ensuring this data is handled ethically and securely is essential to maintaining public trust in robotic systems.

Moreover, robots' autonomy raises complex ethical questions, particularly concerning their decisions in critical situations. Accountability for these decisions, especially when they lead to adverse outcomes, is a contentious issue that requires careful consideration. Additionally, biases in AI systems can lead to discriminatory outcomes, further complicating the ethics of robotics.

Addressing these challenges and considerations remains crucial as we continue to explore the evolution of Generative AI in robotics. Ensuring the reliability, safety, and ethical deployment of AI-driven robots is essential for their practical application and acceptance by society. As these technologies advance, they promise to revolutionize numerous industries, enhancing capabilities and transforming human-robot interaction.

As we close this exploration of Generative AI in business and industry, it becomes clear that while AI brings efficiency and innovation, it works best when paired with human oversight and creativity. This partnership, guided by ethical practices and a commitment to quality, sets the stage for a new era of content creation that is not only automated but, more importantly, inspired. Now, let us turn our attention to the next chapter, where we will examine the transformative impact of AI in another dynamic field: education. Here, technology and human interaction open new avenues for connection and engagement, reshaping how we communicate and interact in the digital world.

6. USING GENERATIVE AI FOR EDUCATIONAL PURPOSES

The illiterate of the 21st century will not be those who can not read and write but those who cannot learn, unlearn and relearn.[1]

— ALVIN TOFFLER

Alvin Toffler's prescient observation highlights the critical importance of adaptability in the rapidly evolving area of education. Generative AI is the key to fostering such adaptability, offering personalized and dynamic learning experiences that meet the diverse needs of students across the globe. By enabling continuous learning tailored to individual pace and style, Generative AI embodies the essence of being able to learn, unlearn, and relearn, which Toffler deemed essential for success in the 21st century.

Imagine entering a classroom where every lesson, content, and assessment is perfectly tailored to your learning style and pace. This vision,

---

1. Toffler, A. (1970). *Future Shock*. Random House

once a mere figment of the educational futurist's imagination, is rapidly becoming a reality with the advent of Generative AI in academic settings. This technology is revolutionizing how we approach learning, making it more personalized, dynamic, and engaging. As we explore the intricacies of how Generative AI is transforming educational experiences, it becomes clear that this technology is not just a tool for efficiency but a catalyst for creating more inclusive and effective learning environments.

CUSTOMIZING LEARNING EXPERIENCES WITH AI

Educational paradigms are shifting profoundly as Generative AI makes it possible to customize learning experiences to unprecedented levels of individualization. Each student comes with unique abilities, learning styles, and pace, which traditional educational models can struggle to accommodate simultaneously. Generative AI steps into this gap by enabling the creation of personalized learning paths. This technology utilizes algorithms to analyze a student's past performance, learning behaviors, and emotional responses to tailor educational content that suits their needs and goals. For instance, if a student excels in visual learning but struggles with textual information, AI systems can automatically present more content in visual formats such as charts, videos, and infographics, enhancing comprehension and retention.

Moreover, the dynamism of AI in education is showcased in its ability to adjust the difficulty of content in real time. As AI continually assesses a student's interaction with learning materials, it can identify when the content could be more challenging or more challenging. The system then adjusts the complexity of the upcoming content to maintain an optimal challenge level, keeping the student in a state of flow. This dynamic adjustment helps maintain a delicate balance where the content is neither overwhelming nor under-stimulating, fostering better learning outcomes and keeping frustration at bay.

Engagement and motivation are critical in educational settings, and here, too, Generative AI introduces transformative strategies. Through gamification and interactive content, AI systems make learning more engaging and fun. These systems can integrate game-like elements such as points, badges, and leaderboards into educational activities or present simulations that allow students to experiment and learn from interactive scenarios. This approach makes learning more enjoyable and encourages students to engage deeper with the material, enhancing motivation and educational endurance.

Feedback and assessment are integral to the learning process, providing students and educators with vital insights into progress and areas needing improvement. Generative AI revolutionizes this aspect by providing immediate, actionable feedback. Unlike traditional methods where feedback can be delayed, AI systems can assess a student's responses in real time and provide instant feedback. This immediacy helps students understand their mistakes and learn from them immediately, greatly enhancing the educational experience. Additionally, AI-driven assessments can help educators understand each student's progress and tailor further instruction to meet the student's specific needs, thereby supporting a more targeted teaching approach.

Visual Element: Interactive AI Learning Model

An interactive diagram illustrates how dynamic content adjustment works further. This model allows you to input different student profiles and see how the AI adjusts the educational content in real time based on various performance metrics. This visualization enhances your understanding of the process and demonstrates the practical application of AI in dynamically tailoring educational content.

Generative AI technology in education sets the stage for a future where learning is not just a process but a highly personalized experience shaped by each student's unique needs and potential. Through its ability to customize learning experiences, adjust content dynamically, enhance engagement, and provide immediate feedback, Generative AI is enhancing educational practices and revolutionizing them, promising a future where every learner can achieve their maximum potential.

GENERATIVE AI AS A TUTORING TOOL

In education, the introduction of AI-powered tutoring systems marks a significant leap towards personalized learning, providing one-on-one instruction that adapts to the individual needs of each student. These systems represent a new era where technology and education converge to offer tailored educational support that can mimic, and in some cases surpass, the benefits of traditional human tutoring. AI tutors are designed to interact with students responsively, adjusting the complexity and pace of instruction in real time to suit the learner's status and progress. This personalized approach helps create a supportive learning environment that can address various learning styles and preferences.

AI-powered tutoring systems are particularly adept at identifying learning gaps. Through continuous assessment and interaction, these systems can pinpoint specific areas where a student may struggle and immediately intervene with targeted exercises. For example, suppose a student consistently encounters difficulties with particular math problems. In that case, the AI tutor can recognize these challenges and provide customized practice problems focusing on underlying concepts or skills that need reinforcement. This capability ensures that students receive immediate attention in trouble areas, significantly improving learning efficiency and mastery of material.

Moreover, the impact of AI in language learning through these tutoring systems is profound. AI tutors can engage students in conversation practice and pronunciation correction, making language learning more interactive and practical. These systems can use speech recognition to analyze a student's pronunciation, offering real-time corrective feedback that helps improve language skills quickly and effectively. Additionally, AI tutors can simulate various conversational scenarios, from casual chatting to formal interviews, providing practical language use cases that enhance students' ability to use the language in real-world situations. This hands-on approach to language learning boosts confidence and accelerates the learning process.

Accessibility and inclusion are perhaps among the most transformative aspects of AI tutoring systems. By providing high-quality educational support through digital platforms, these systems make learning accessible to students in remote or underserved areas who might not have access to qualified human tutors. AI tutoring can bridge the educational divide by delivering consistent, personalized, and engaging instruction to students regardless of geographical location. This democratization of education is pivotal in leveling the playing field, ensuring that every student has the opportunity to achieve their personalized educational goals and expand their knowledge and skills.

As we continue to explore AI's capabilities and applications in tutoring, it becomes increasingly clear that these intelligent systems are not just supplementary tools but foundational elements in crafting future educational frameworks that are inclusive, effective, and deeply personalized.

THE ROLE OF AI IN LANGUAGE LEARNING

Integrating Artificial Intelligence, specifically through NLP, has initiated a transformative shift in language learning. NLP allows AI to interpret, understand, and generate meaningful and relevant human language. This capability is pivotal in creating interactive language learning experiences that are deeply immersive and highly effective. When you engage with an AI-driven language learning application, you're not merely interacting with a static program that delivers pre-set phrases and sentences. Instead, you're experiencing a dynamic platform that analyzes your inputs, understands the context, and responds in a way that mimics a human language tutor.

The sophisticated algorithms behind NLP enable AI to break down the language learning process into manageable, intuitive pieces. For instance, the AI assesses your grammar, syntax, and semantics in real time when constructing sentences in a new language. It then provides instant feedback, correcting mistakes and explaining them in a manner you can easily understand. This immediate and personalized feedback loop is crucial for effective learning, as it allows you to learn from errors and improve continuously without feeling discouraged.

Furthermore, integrating cultural context into language learning is another area where AI shines. Understanding a language involves more than just grasping vocabulary and grammar; it also requires an appreciation of the cultural nuances and contexts in which the language operates. AI-driven programs can simulate real-life scenarios that embed cultural nuances, from ordering food in a Parisian café to negotiating business terms in a Tokyo boardroom. These simulations are enriched with cultural insights, helping you learn the language and understand its gestures, formalities, and social norms. This holistic approach enhances language comprehension and significantly boosts your fluency and confidence in using the language in appropriate cultural contexts.

Speech recognition technology in AI further enhances the language learning experience by providing real-time feedback on pronunciation and intonation—crucial aspects often overlooked in traditional language learning settings. This technology uses advanced algorithms to analyze your speech patterns, compare them with native pronunciations, and offer corrective feedback immediately. Whether you are practicing simple greetings or complex dialogues, the AI continuously assesses your speech, helping to refine your accent and improve your spoken language skills effectively. This aspect of AI is particularly beneficial for learners who may not have regular access to native speakers, as it provides a reliable and accessible means of practicing and improving pronunciation.

Lastly, AI's personalization of learning materials marks a significant advancement in educational technology. As AI systems learn more about your proficiency level, learning pace, and preferences, they can custom-tailor the academic content to match your specific learning needs. This might involve emphasizing vocabulary you struggle with or presenting grammar lessons in the most engaging formats, such as through interactive games or story-based modules. This level of personalization ensures that the learning process remains relevant to your individual needs, significantly enhancing both the efficiency and enjoyment of learning a new language.

As AI continues to evolve, its expanding role in language learning will break down more barriers and create opportunities for a more connected and linguistically diverse world. The potential of AI-driven language learning tools to tailor educational experiences to individual needs, integrate cultural nuances, provide instant feedback, and personalize learning materials presents a new era in language education that embraces technology not as a mere supplement but as a pivotal component of the learning experience.

AI-GENERATED EDUCATIONAL CONTENT: PROS AND CONS

In an era where educational demands are continuously evolving, the advent of AI in generating educational content—ranging from digital textbooks to interactive learning modules—represents a significant leap forward in educational technology. This technology's capacity to automate and innovate content creation transforms pedagogical approaches, allowing educational materials to be more dynamic and tailored to diverse learning environments. AI-driven systems can analyze vast amounts of academic data, identify trends and gaps in knowledge, and generate content that addresses these gaps with precision. For instance, in areas where students struggle, AI can produce additional quizzes and explanatory content to reinforce learning, ensuring that resources are abundant, targeted, and effective.

However, while the benefits are substantial, they come with challenges. One of the primary concerns about AI-generated educational content is its quality and reliability. Given the nuances involved in academic content, the fear that AI might oversimplify complex concepts or generate inaccurate information is valid. Ensuring that AI systems are trained on high-quality, accurate data is crucial. Moreover, the algorithms must be sophisticated enough to handle the complexities of educational subjects while maintaining the depth and rigor required for effective learning. Regular audits and updates to the AI systems are necessary to maintain the integrity and accuracy of the content generated.

The scalability and accessibility that AI brings to content creation are perhaps among its most significant advantages. Traditional content creation is often a slow, labor-intensive process that can need help to keep pace with rapid educational standards and knowledge changes. AI dramatically accelerates this process, enabling educational content to be updated or created in real time as new information becomes available or curriculum standards evolve. This capability ensures learners can access the most current information, making it easier to distribute high-quality educational resources to a broader audience. AI-generated content can be a game-changer for regions or populations with scarce educational resources, democratizing access to information and leveling the academic playing field across diverse socio-economic strata.

Ethical considerations also play an essential role in integrating AI into content generation. The potential for bias in AI-generated materials is a significant concern, as it can influence educational outcomes and perpetuate inequalities. Algorithms trained on biased data sets can produce content that reflects these biases, subtly influencing the knowledge and perspectives that students acquire. To combat this, employing diverse datasets and implementing algorithmic checks that identify and mitigate biases is essential. Additionally, the risk of misinformation—whether through error or manipulation—necessitates stringent verification processes for AI-generated content, ensuring that the information provided to learners is timely but also trustworthy and balanced.

Navigating these challenges requires a thoughtful approach to integrating AI in content creation, one that balances the benefits of technology with a commitment to maintaining educational quality and ethical standards. As we continue to harness AI's potential in education, it becomes increasingly clear that this technology is not just a tool for efficiency but a transformative force that can reshape how we create, deliver, and engage with educational content.

In conclusion, AI-generated educational content holds immense promise for transforming learning experiences through customization, scalability, and accessibility. However, realizing this potential fully necessitates addressing the challenges of quality assurance, ethical considerations, and the prevention of misinformation. As we advance into the next chapter, we will explore AI's broader impacts on society, probing its capabilities and the responsibilities of integrating such a powerful technology into our daily lives and institutional frameworks.

DISPELLING FEAR

Ignorance is the parent of fear.

— HERMAN MELVILLE (MOBY-DICK)

There's a lot of fear about AI, and understandably so. It's natural to fear anything we don't know about... and what's the solution? *To find out about it.* This is something applicable to all areas of life – there's so much hate out there born out of fear of the unknown, and if we could address all of our fears by seeking to understand, the world would be a much better place. In the case of AI, this is much more straightforward than many people realize, but there's so much noise about it out there that it's not always easy to get a clear picture.

The goal of this book is to explain generative AI to everyone from the complete beginner to the technological explorer who wants to know more – and that's why we started with the basics of AI and how it evolved to be what it is today. Understanding something fully means getting to its roots and building our knowledge from there. Once we understand it, it stops being something to fear, and we start to see its enormous potential and how we can tailor its use to suit our needs.

When my son introduced me to ChatGTP, my whole perspective on AI changed, and I realized just how much potential it has. But I also know how skeptical I was at first, and how I needed to bridge the gap in my understanding, so I want to help more people to do the same – because AI is here to stay, and it's something we can all use to bring us closer to our goals... It isn't something to fear.

Now that you have a deeper understanding of generative AI, I'd like to ask for your help. All you need to do to bring this understanding to more people is write a short review.

By leaving a review of this book on Amazon, you'll show new readers how they can sidestep the noise, and find the understanding they're looking for.

With so much information available online, much of it of dubious quality, reviews are essential for helping people find the resources that will truly help them. It may not feel like much to you, but it makes a huge difference.

Thank you so much for your support. AI is a powerful tool with huge potential; let's remove the fear, and find out what we can really do with it.

Scan the QR code below

7. CREATIVE EXPRESSIONS THROUGH GENERATIVE AI

The only way to discover the limits of the possible is to go beyond them into the impossible.[1]

— ARTHUR CLARKE

This quote by renowned science fiction writer Clarke resonates with the spirit of pushing creative boundaries through technology. As we examine how Generative AI redefines art, music, and literature, this sentiment underscores the journey from the conceivable to groundbreaking artistic innovation.

Imagine a canvas where the colors blend not from the traditional brush strokes of a human artist but from the algorithmic interpretations of machine learning to feel and create. Generative AI is reshaping what it means to make art, challenging our traditional perceptions, and inviting seasoned artists and newcomers alike to explore an expanding universe of creativity. This chapter examines

---

1. https://www.resourcefulmanager.com/innovation-quotes/

how Generative AI serves as both a tool and a partner in the art world, democratizing creativity and opening new areas of artistic expression that were unimaginable just a few years ago.

EXPLORING DIGITAL ART WITH AI

Collaborative Art Creation

Generative AI is a tool and collaborator in digital art, bringing a new dimension to artistic creation. Artists, traditionally confined to the limitations of human imagination and physical skill, are now embracing AI to push beyond these boundaries. By inputting initial ideas, themes, or emotions into AI systems, artists can collaborate with algorithms that process and reinterpret these inputs to generate novel artistic outputs. This process creates a dynamic interplay between human intention and machine interpretation, creating artworks that might never have been conceived by human minds alone. For instance, consider an artist focusing on climate change; by feeding the AI system relevant data and images, the AI can produce visual interpretations that highlight the impacts of climate change in ways that resonate more profoundly with viewers.

AI in Artistic Inspiration and Conceptualization

Generative AI is also pivotal in art's inspiration and conceptualization phases. Artists often use AI algorithms to generate ideas, themes, and visual elements that provide fresh perspectives and inspire new directions for their work. AI systems can analyze vast arrays of historical art, extracting underlying themes and styles and recombining these elements in novel ways. This capability speeds up the creative process and introduces artists to a broader spectrum of artistic expressions and styles they might not have encountered otherwise.

For example, an AI analyzing the works of impressionist and surrealist artists might blend these styles to create a new form of expression that sparks new ideas in an artist's mind.

The Democratization of Art

One of the most significant impacts of Generative AI in the art world is its ability to democratize art creation. Individuals may need formal art training with AI tools to create complex, aesthetically pleasing artworks. These tools often come with user-friendly interfaces that guide users through the creative process, making art creation accessible to everyone. By lowering the barriers to entry, AI is opening the art world, allowing more people to express themselves creatively and participate in cultural production. This democratization not only diversifies the types of art being produced but also enriches the cultural diaspora with a broader range of voices and perspectives.

Ethical Considerations and Originality

However, the integration of AI in art is not without its ethical considerations, particularly concerning originality and copyright. As AI-generated artworks become more prevalent, questions arise about the originality of art created with or by AI. Who holds the copyright to an AI-generated piece—the artist who designed the initial input, the programmers who created the AI, or the AI itself? These questions challenge existing legal frameworks and demand new considerations about authorship and creative rights in the digital age. Furthermore, there is an ongoing debate about the authenticity of AI art and whether it can be considered 'creative' since it depends on algorithms and machine data. These discussions are crucial as they shape the evolving norms and ethics surrounding digital art creation.

Visual Element: Interactive AI Art Gallery

Consider exploring an interactive online AI art gallery to further your understanding and appreciation of AI-generated art. This platform allows you to view a diverse array of artworks created by AI, offering insights into the techniques and algorithms used to produce them. As you engage with this digital gallery, reflect on your perceptions of art and creativity in the age of AI. What does it mean for a piece to be created by AI, and how does it change your experience as a viewer? This interactive exploration enhances your appreciation of AI-generated art and invites you to ponder the broader implications of technology in creative expression.

THE NEW WAVE OF AI-GENERATED MUSIC

In music production, the role of Generative AI has transitioned from merely experimental to fundamentally transformative. AI algorithms can now compose music, generate lyrics, and even produce complete musical pieces that resonate deeply with human emotions and cultural nuances. This technological evolution is not just about automating music creation; it's about opening new avenues for creativity and expression in the music industry. AI's ability to analyze vast music datasets allows it to learn from existing compositions, drawing on various styles and genres to create something entirely new and often unexpected.

Consider the process of composition where AI can now take the lead. By inputting basic parameters such as tempo, scale, and genre, musicians can leverage AI to compose complex pieces of music that might take a human composer much longer to conceptualize. This collaboration between human musicians and AI continues beyond mere composition. AI extends its capabilities to lyrical creation, analyzing popular themes and vocabulary from existing songs to generate fitting lyrics for new compositions. This fusion of AI's analytical prowess with human creative insight is producing compelling music that pushes conventional boundaries.

AI's influence stretches further into music production, where it adjusts sound levels, harmonizes melodies, and even suggests changes to improve the overall quality of the track. These advancements represent a significant shift in how music is produced, making high-quality music production more accessible to artists without the means to hire large production teams. This democratization of music production tools has the potential to level the playing field, allowing emerging artists from diverse backgrounds to share their voices and stories.

The integration of AI in music has also sparked notable collabora-tions that highlight its potential to revolutionize the industry. For instance, in events like the Eurovision Song Contest, AI has composed songs that reflect a blend of styles from participating countries, creating a unique musical experience that celebrates cultural diversity. Similarly, albums where AI plays a significant role in composition and production are becoming more prevalent, show-casing AI's growing influence in the music industry.

However, the rise of AI-generated music also brings to light several challenges that need careful consideration. Issues related to copyright of AI-generated compositions are increasingly coming to the fore-front. As AI blurs the lines between creator and tool, the music industry must rethink copyright laws to consider who the rightful owner of an AI-generated piece is: the programmer, the artist, or the AI itself. This question becomes even more complicated when AI independently creates music that resembles existing copyrighted works, potentially leading to legal disputes.

Moreover, the authenticity and role of human creativity in AI-gener-ated music are topics of intense debate. While AI can enhance the music creation process, there is a concern that over-reliance on AI could diminish the value of human creativity in music. Critics argue that music, at its core, is an expression of human experience and emotion, something that AI might only partially replicate. Therefore, maintaining a balance where AI is seen as a tool rather than a replacement for human creativity is crucial.

As we navigate this new era of AI-generated music, we must foster an environment where technology enhances creativity without overshadowing the human elements that make music profoundly touching and inherently human. This ongoing evolution in music production and composition heralds a new age of artistic expression, where technology and creativity merge to explore uncharted territories of musical artistry.

WRITING WITH AI: NOVELS, SCRIPTS, AND BEYOND

In creative writing, the advent of Generative AI is like a new muse that inspires and actively participates in the creative process. From novelists to scriptwriters, writers find AI a powerful ally capable of generating novel ideas, intricate plotlines, and even fully realized characters. This collaboration often begins with the writer inputting essential narrative elements—themes, character traits, or a storyline outline—and the AI expanding these into rich, detailed plots or suggesting developments that bring unexpected depth and twists to the narrative.

Consider the scenario where a writer is crafting a historical novel. By feeding the AI historical data, themes of the era, key events, and character outlines, the AI can suggest dialogue authentic to the period, plot elements based on historical incidents, or character interactions that reflect the social norms of that era. This enriches the writer's work and saves significant research time, allowing the writer to focus on refining the story's emotional resonance and narrative pace. In this partnership, AI acts not as a mere tool but a co-creator that brings a wealth of data-driven insights and novel interpretations to the creative table.

Moreover, AI's role in creative writing is seen as a collaborative force that enhances human creativity rather than replacing it. Writers utilize AI to break through creative blocks or explore narrative possibilities they might have yet to consider. For instance, an AI might suggest a subplot that introduces a new conflict, adding complexity and depth to the main storyline, or propose character backstories that provide new layers to their motivations. This collaborative process can be remarkably liberating for writers, offering them various creative paths and possibilities that enrich their original vision without detracting from their artistic authority.

The impact of AI-generated literature is beginning to ripple through the publishing industry, challenging traditional norms and practices. Publishers are exploring AI tools to predict market trends and reader preferences, helping them make more informed decisions about which books to support and promote. Additionally, AI is starting to play a role in editing and proofreading processes, streamlining these tasks to allow faster turnaround times without compromising quality. However, the most disruptive aspect of AI in publishing may be the potential to change how stories are told and consumed. AI-generated interactive novels, where readers can choose different plot developments, are becoming more feasible and popular, potentially leading to a significant shift in narrative structures and storytelling techniques.

However, the use of AI in writing is full of ethical considerations. Questions of authorship and originality are at the forefront of AI-assisted literature debates. When a significant portion of a novel's content is generated by AI, determining the rightful author—or authors—becomes complex. Is it the human who provided the initial input and guidance, the developers of the AI, or some combination thereof? This question complicates copyright discussions and challenges our traditional understanding of creative ownership. Moreover, the risk of homogenization in literature, where AI models might produce stylistically similar works based on what is most popular or marketable, raises concerns about the diversity and richness of literary culture.

As we navigate this new era of literary creation, it becomes evident that AI is not just a tool but a transformative force in creative writing. Its ability to collaborate closely with human writers, enhancing their creativity and broadening their narrative possibilities, heralding a future where storytelling can evolve in unprecedented ways. But as we embrace these new opportunities, we must also navigate ethics with care, ensuring that AI enhances human creativity without compromising the values and principles underpinning the literary world.

AI-DRIVEN DESIGN IN FASHION

In the dynamic world of fashion, where trends are as fleeting as they are influential, Generative AI is beginning to carve its niche, revolutionizing how designs come to life and how they are consumed. Fashion designers, often seen as the vanguard of creativity and innovation, are now harnessing AI to predict and set trends, creating garments that resonate deeply with consumer desires yet remain ahead of the curve. This blend of technology and fashion accelerates the design process and introduces a level of personalization previously unattainable in this industry.

AI in Fashion Design

Generative AI's role in fashion design extends beyond mere automation; it involves intricate processes where AI analyzes current fashion trends, consumer behavior, and social media data to forecast upcoming trends. This predictive capability allows designers to stay ahead, crafting collections that align closely with future consumer preferences. For instance, AI can scan vast amounts of data from fashion shows, online retail sites, and style blogs to identify patterns gaining traction. Using this information, designers can create pieces that are both innovative and in demand. Moreover, AI-driven tools assist designers in visualizing and simulating how different fabrics and cuts work together, significantly speeding up the creative process and reducing material waste during prototyping.

Customization and Personalization

The advent of AI in fashion also brings unprecedented customization and personalization. Generative AI enables brands to offer personalized shopping experiences by suggesting items based on a customer's past shopping habits, social media activity, and even current trends. For instance, an AI system might analyze a customer's preference for minimalist style and recommend garments that match this aesthetic from new collections. Beyond just recommendations, AI is used to create custom-designed pieces. Customers can input their preferences or moods into an AI interface, which generates clothing designs tailored to these inputs. Such personalization enhances customer satisfaction and fosters a deeper connection between the brand and its clientele, as consumers see their styles and preferences reflected in the products they purchase.

Intellectual Property Issues

However, the integration of AI in fashion design has challenges, particularly in intellectual property ("IP") rights. The question of who owns a design created by AI—whether it's the programmer who designed the AI, the fashion designer who used it, or potentially the AI itself—remains largely unresolved. Recent legal discussions and court cases have begun to tackle these issues, but technological development in AI often outstrips the slower pace of legal systems. Furthermore, there are ethical considerations regarding the originality of AI-generated designs. As AI tools become more widespread, distinguishing between human-created and AI-generated designs becomes more complex, potentially leading to conflicts over copyright and the true nature of creativity in fashion.

This fashion industry transformation through Generative AI opens many possibilities, from how we conceive and create new garments to how we interact with consumers. AI's blend of human creativity and algorithmic precision for designers and brands promises to redefine current practices and lead the fashion industry into a new era of innovation and personalization. As we move forward, the continued evolution of AI tools will likely introduce more sophisticated applications, further blurring the lines between technology and traditional fashion design and challenging our perceptions of creativity and machine collaboration.

In summary, this chapter has explored the transformative impact of Generative AI in creative writing, highlighting its role as both a collaborator and an innovator. As we move forward, it's clear that the integration of AI in literature is reshaping how stories are written and consumed and how they are valued and understood in our culture. Looking ahead, the next chapter will explore the ethical implications and societal impacts of Generative AI across various sectors, ensuring that as we advance technologically, we remain anchored by a solid moral foundation.

8. ETHICAL CONSIDERATIONS AND SOCIETAL IMPACT

An AI Acceptable Usage Policy (AUP) provides organizations with a framework for the ethical and responsible deployment of artificial intelligence.[1]

— MARY CARMICHAEL

This quote underscores organizations' need to carefully navigate the integration of generative AI within their operations. It discusses the various ethical dilemmas and societal impacts of deploying AI technologies. You might explore how different sectors implement these frameworks to balance innovation with ethical considerations, reflecting on how this approach can serve as a model for responsible AI usage across industries.

As Generative AI's complexity continues to evolve, the shimmering promise of technology is occasionally shadowed by profound ethical questions and societal implications. Picture a world where AI

---

1. https://www.isaca.org/resources/news-and-trends/newsletters/atisaca/2023/volume-44/key-considerations-for-developing-organizational-generative-ai-policies

enhances productivity and shapes our society's cultural and social fabric. In this chapter, we explore the nuanced terrain of AI ethics, focusing on the critical issue of bias and fairness, the influence of AI on societal norms, and the global discourse on ethical AI practices. This exploration is about understanding AI's potential pitfalls and fortifying our commitment to responsibly using this powerful tool.

UNDERSTANDING AI BIAS AND FAIRNESS

Sources of Bias

At the heart of the challenges associated with Generative AI lies the issue of bias, which can inadvertently arise from various sources. One primary source is the data used to train AI systems. Since AI learns to make decisions based on this data, any inherent biases in the data—stemming from historical inequalities or skewed representation—can lead to biased AI behavior. For instance, if an AI system is trained predominantly on medical data from one ethnic group, it might be less accurate in diagnosing conditions in people from other ethnic backgrounds. Similarly, AI used in hiring processes might replicate past hiring biases if the historical data it learns from contains such biases.

Algorithmic Details Behind Bias

Understanding how biases are encoded in AI algorithms requires a dive into the technical underpinnings of these systems. AI models are built on complex mathematical and statistical principles, which determine how input data is processed and interpreted. Bias can creep into this process at multiple stages—from how data is collected and selected to the assumptions embedded in the algorithms that analyze this data. For example, the weighting of variables in decision-making processes can disproportionately affect the outcome, favoring specific groups over others based on the criteria set by the algorithm's design.

Impact on Society

The ramifications of AI bias are profound, as they can perpetuate and even amplify social inequalities and discrimination. In sectors like law enforcement, biased AI can lead to unfair profiling of specific demographics, while in lending, it can prevent marginalized groups from accessing financial services. The societal impact of such biases is not just a matter of individual injustice but can lead to broader social divisions and erode trust in AI technologies.

Mitigating Bias

Addressing AI bias involves a multifaceted approach, including diversifying training data, developing algorithms to identify and correct biases, and maintaining transparency in AI decision-making processes. Employing diverse datasets representing different groups ensures that AI systems can learn more equitably. Furthermore, developing algorithms that specifically monitor for and correct biases can help mitigate these issues. Transparency is equally crucial, as it allows users to understand how AI makes decisions and on what basis, fostering greater trust and accountability.

Misconceptions

A common misconception is that AI is inherently objective. This belief can dangerously obscure the realities of AI bias, leading to an underestimation of the ethical challenges involved in AI deployment. Dispelling this myth is crucial, as recognizing the subjective elements in AI training and function is the first step toward addressing ethical concerns.

Ethical Frameworks

Developing and implementing robust ethical frameworks is essential for guiding the equitable use of Generative AI. These frameworks should address technical aspects of bias mitigation and consider the broader ethical implications of AI applications. They serve as a blueprint for developers, users, and policymakers, ensuring that AI is used in ways that respect human rights and promote fairness.

Global Perspective on AI Ethics

Different cultures and countries approach the ethics of AI from various perspectives, influenced by local values, legal systems, and societal norms. Understanding these diverse viewpoints is vital for developing globally relevant AI solutions that respect cultural differences while upholding universal ethical standards. For instance, European approaches to AI regulation often emphasize privacy and data protection, while other regions might prioritize innovation and economic growth.

Case Studies of Ethical AI Deployment

Real-world examples provide invaluable insights into ethical AI deployment's practical challenges and successes. Companies across industries increasingly prioritize ethical AI, implementing systems that comply with legal standards and align with ethical best practices. For example, a tech company might share its framework for ethical AI in product development, detailing how it assesses potential biases and the measures it takes to mitigate them. These case studies illustrate the practical applications of ethical guidelines and highlight companies' ongoing challenges in ensuring AI ethics are deeply integrated into their operations.

Interactive Element: Ethical AI Checklist

To further engage with the concept of ethical AI, here is an interactive checklist that you can use to assess AI tools and applications:

Here are some questions to ask yourself as well as employing the interactive checklist from the website above:

- Does the AI application use diverse and representative data?
- Are there measures in place to identify and correct biases?
- Is there transparency in how the AI makes decisions?
- Are there ethical guidelines governing the use of AI?
- How does the AI application impact different demographic groups?

This checklist can serve as a starting point for evaluating AI applications, encouraging a deeper consideration of how these technologies are developed and used in various sectors. Whether you are a developer, a business leader, or a concerned citizen, understanding and applying these principles is crucial for fostering ethical AI.

PRIVACY AND SECURITY IN THE AGE OF GENERATIVE AI

In an era where Generative AI weaves through the fabric of our digital day, the sanctity of personal privacy assumes a pivotal role. As these technologies become deeply integrated into our society, understanding and safeguarding privacy becomes a preference and necessity. The profound capabilities of Generative AI to transform vast datasets into actionable insights and personalized experiences also come with the potential to intrude into our personal lives, making the protection of privacy a complex yet critical challenge. This challenge is particularly pronounced in the evolving legal field, exemplified by robust initiatives like the EU's Artificial Intelligence Act and the USA's AI Bill of Rights. These frameworks are not static; they are dynamic responses to the rapid advancements in AI, designed to set benchmarks for privacy and security while protecting an environment where technological innovation can thrive responsibly.

The privacy paradox presents a peculiar dilemma for Generative AI. This paradox encapsulates the conflict between leveraging data to fuel AI advancements and the imperative to protect individual privacy. Every interaction with digital platforms, whether shopping online, using social media, or driving through an intelligent city, feeds data into AI systems that improve services and user experiences. However, this data also includes personal information that, if mishandled, can lead to privacy violations. Real-world examples abound where organizations have grappled with this paradox. Some have successfully navigated these waters by implementing stringent data handling and processing protocols that enhance user trust and adherence to global data protection regulations. Others have faltered, leading to breaches compromising personal data and eroding public confidence in AI technologies.

Navigating the complex terrain of data protection laws like **General Data Protection Regulation ("GDPR")**

in Europe and **California Consumer Privacy Act of 2018 ("CCPP")**

in California reveals the intricate balance these regulations seek to achieve. These laws provide a framework for data protection that includes rights to access, correct, and delete personal data, reflecting a growing recognition of privacy as a fundamental human right. However, applying these laws in the context of AI poses unique challenges. AI developers often find themselves in a bind, trying to comply with these stringent regulations while pushing the boundaries of what AI can achieve. For instance, using AI in predictive policing or behavioral advertising can raise significant privacy concerns that are only sometimes adequately addressed by existing laws. Compliance, therefore, is not just about adhering to legal standards but also about embracing the spirit of these regulations, which aim to protect individuals from invasive data practices.

To safeguard privacy in AI applications, several strategic measures can be implemented. Anonymization and data masking are techniques designed to protect user identity, even as data is used to train AI models. Federated learning offers another layer of security, allowing AI to learn from decentralized data sources without centralizing sensitive information. These methods are complemented by adopting blockchain and advanced encryption technologies, which provide robust security for data transactions involved in AI processes. By integrating these technologies, developers can enhance the security of AI systems, making it harder for unauthorized entities to access or misuse personal data.

Emerging concerns in AI privacy include the risks posed by synthetic data and the potential creation of deep fakes. These technologies, while innovative, open new avenues for privacy violations and misinformation. To counter these risks, ongoing research and the development of enhanced detection technologies are crucial. Experts in privacy law and AI technology advocate for a proactive approach to these emerging challenges, emphasizing the need for continuous innovation in privacy-preserving technologies and the adaptation of regulatory frameworks to address new vulnerabilities.

In-depth case studies provide a real-world perspective on how organizations navigate the complexities of privacy in AI-driven projects. For instance, a healthcare company, Docus.ai[2], which utilizes AI to analyze patient data for personalized treatment plans, faces significant privacy challenges. Docus.ai complies with strict healthcare regulations and builds patient trust by implementing a comprehensive framework that includes data anonymization, secure data storage,

2. Thoughtful. (n.d.). AI in medicine: Transforming patient treatment and care. Retrieved from www.thoughtful.ai

and transparent patient consent processes. This case study highlights the practical applications of privacy measures and underscores the ongoing challenges in balancing innovation with ethical considerations in using Generative AI.

THE FUTURE OF WORK: NAVIGATING GENERATIVE AI AND EMPLOYMENT

Employment shaped by Generative AI presents a dichotomy of disruption and opportunity. This technology's influence extends beyond mere automation, fundamentally transforming job markets and necessitating a shift in the skills that define professional competence. As you find yourself in this transitioning job ecosystem, understanding these changes and preparing for the emerging realities is crucial. Generative AI, while streamlining operations and creating new efficiencies, also poses challenges such as job displacement. However, it simultaneously catalyzes the creation of new roles requiring an evolved skill set. For instance, as AI takes over routine data-processing tasks, the demand for roles that oversee AI operations, ensure ethical applications, and manage AI-driven systems is on the rise. These roles often require technical skills and a deep understanding of how AI interacts within broader business and ethical contexts.

The job market's evolution is tightly interwoven with the skills that future workforces need to thrive. Critical thinking, creativity, and AI literacy are indispensable skills in an AI-driven future. Critical thinking is essential, as it empowers you to make strategic decisions and solve complex problems that AI cannot address alone. Creativity, too, gains prominence, not just in artistic professions but across various sectors, as it enables the innovation of new solutions and the reimagining of existing processes. Meanwhile, AI literacy is more than just desirable; it is necessary. Understanding AI and its applications in one's field will allow you to work effectively alongside AI systems and leverage these tools to enhance productivity and innovation.

In this rapidly changing employment environment, the importance of lifelong learning cannot be overstated. The agility to learn and adapt to new technologies and processes is pivotal. Continuous education and training become integral to staying relevant and competitive in the workforce. Employers and educational institutions play a critical role here, facilitating ongoing learning opportunities that help individuals respond to technological advancements and industry demands. For example, tech companies often provide training sessions on the latest AI tools and methodologies, allowing their employees to stay at the cutting edge of technology applications.

Ethical deployment of AI in the workplace is another critical consideration. As AI systems become more integral to business operations, ensuring these systems are used fairly and transparently is paramount. This includes being transparent about AI decisions, ensuring AI systems do not perpetuate biases, and maintaining a workplace culture that values human decision-making and accountability. Worker engagement in AI deployments also matters, as it fosters a workplace where employees feel valued and part of the transition rather than sidelined by technology. For instance, involving employees in AI projects' development and deployment phases can help identify potential issues early and align AI strategies with worker needs and ethical standards.

Navigating the future of work with Generative AI involves a balance of embracing technological advancements and mitigating their disruptive impacts. As AI reshapes industries, the readiness to adapt, the continuous pursuit of relevant skills, and a firm commitment to ethical practices will define the success of individuals and organizations. In this dynamic scenario, the potential of AI to serve as a powerful ally in the workplace hinges on our collective ability to steer its application towards enhancing both business outcomes and human values. As we progress deeper into this era of technological integration, fostering an environment where AI and human capabilities complement each other will be crucial in realizing the full potential of this technology.

SOCIO-ECONOMIC EQUITY AND FAIRNESS

In the dynamic interplay of technology and society, Generative AI holds transformative potential, yet it poses significant challenges to socio-economic equity. Socio-economic equity in the context of AI involves designing systems that enhance efficiencies and distribute the benefits of AI technologies across all segments of society, avoiding exacerbating existing disparities. This equitable approach necessitates a deep understanding of how AI impacts diverse socio-economic groups, accompanied by a commitment to ensuring that these technologies are developed and deployed to promote fairness and inclusiveness.

Generative AI's impact on different socio-economic groups is multifaceted, offering numerous benefits and presenting substantial risks. On the positive side, AI can significantly increase accessibility to essential services such as education, healthcare, and financial services. For instance, AI-driven educational platforms can provide high-quality learning resources to underprivileged areas, breaking geographical and economic barriers that traditionally hindered access to education. Similarly, AI applications in healthcare can offer diagnostic tools and personalized treatment plans previously unavailable in remote or economically disadvantaged regions, potentially transforming health outcomes for those communities.

While promising, introducing AI into various sectors introduces significant challenges, particularly for lower socio-economic groups.

One of the most critical issues is the displacement of jobs due to automation. As AI systems and robots begin to perform routine tasks, sectors that once relied heavily on lower-skilled labor face massive job cuts, deepening unemployment and widening the economic inequality gap. Furthermore, the surge in surveillance technologies raises concerns about privacy breaches, with the less privileged at a higher risk of violating their privacy rights due to limited resources to counter such intrusions. A comprehensive strategy for instilling fairness into AI algorithms is essential to navigate these challenges. This includes conducting thorough audits of algorithms to uncover and rectify biases that could result in unfair outcomes. It is equally important to draw on diverse datasets that mirror the wide range of human experiences, ensuring AI systems do not adopt biases that favor particular groups. Transparency in how AI makes decisions is another pillar of fairness, giving people the clarity to understand, question, and appeal decisions made by AI. Regulation and policy are indispensable in promoting socio-economic equity through AI. Recognizing the potential for harm, governments and international organizations are moving towards regulating AI to safeguard against its adverse effects and guarantee that its benefits reach all layers of society equitably. These regulations are designed to oversee not just the technical execution of AI but also its societal implications, ensuring that AI's application is conscientious and that protective measures are in place for the most vulnerable groups.

Real-world case studies provide substantial insights into the practical application of these principles. Companies like ZestFinance or ZestAI

have pioneered AI to extend fair credit to all. They utilize machine learning to analyze vast amounts of non-traditional data to make credit decisions that are more inclusive for populations typically underserved by traditional credit systems. Another example is the use of AI by Los Angeles, where an AI program was implemented to optimize fire department responses. By analyzing data on emergency calls, the AI system improved response times across all districts, thereby enhancing service delivery in economically disadvantaged areas.

These examples underscore AI's dual potential to bridge or widen socio-economic divides, depending on how it is deployed. They also highlight the ongoing need for vigilance, innovation, and leadership to ensure that AI technologies benefit all segments of society.

SOCIO-ECONOMIC IMPACTS OF GENERATIVE AI

The advent of Generative AI is reshaping the socio-economic strata, profoundly influencing employment trends, educational systems, and social equity. As this technology permeates various sectors, its impacts extend beyond mere automation, fostering new skills and job roles while posing challenges such as job displacement and exacerbating existing inequalities. Understanding these dynamics is essential for understanding the future that Generative AI is helping to shape.

Employment Trends and Job Displacement

Generative AI's capacity to automate complex tasks has led to shifts in the job market, characterized by both the displacement of traditional roles and the creation of new opportunities. In sectors like manufacturing, AI-driven automation has streamlined production processes and reduced the demand for routine manual labor. However, this displacement is often accompanied by the emergence of new roles that require more advanced technical skills, such as AI system supervision, data analysis, and machine maintenance. The retail sector experiences similar shifts, where AI automates inventory management and customer service tasks yet increases demand for IT specialists who can implement and oversee these systems.

The transformation in employment necessitates an agile workforce equipped with skills pertinent to an AI-driven economy. Data literacy, AI supervision, and ethical management skills are becoming indispensable as AI technologies become central to more industries. Leveraging AI capabilities to enhance productivity and innovation is fast becoming a valued skill set across various fields.

Education and Skill Development

The impact of Generative AI on education is multifaceted, influencing not only the content of educational programs but also their delivery. AI's role in personalized learning exemplifies this shift; by adapting educational content to fit individual students' learning paces and styles, AI creates a more inclusive and effective academic environment. This personalization extends to higher education and professional training, where AI systems can design custom curricula that address specific skills gaps, aligning education more closely with industry needs.

However, the rapid evolution of AI also necessitates an evolution in educational curricula to prepare students for the future job market. This evolution involves imparting technical skills related to AI and data science and fostering soft skills such as critical thinking, creativity, and ethical reasoning. These skills are crucial for managing AI systems and making informed decisions in an AI-integrated workplace.

Social Equity Concerns

Generative AI, while heralding a new era of efficiency and innovation, also casts a shadow on the socio-economic fabric by deepening the chasm of social inequality. This divide primarily manifests through the uneven distribution of AI technology and educational resources, allowing the affluent disproportionate access to these transformative tools. The risk is palpable: without strategic interventions to level the playing field, Generative AI could inadvertently become the privilege of the few, leaving behind those in lower socio-economic strata and exacerbating the gulf between the haves and the have-nots. Small enterprises, for example, face significant barriers in integrating AI solutions that could revolutionize their operations due to prohibitive costs and a lack of technical expertise. In contrast, with their abundant resources, more giant corporations are positioned to exploit AI for even greater market dominance, thus widening the competitive gap. A multifaceted approach to policy-making is crucial to mitigate these risks and promote a more equitable socio-economic strata. Key to this endeavor is the democratization of AI, ensuring that the revolutionary benefits of Generative AI are not concentrated among the elite but dispersed across the societal spectrum.

This can be achieved through targeted policies and initiatives: -

- **Public Education Enhancement**: There is a pressing need to invest in and expand public education programs focusing on AI literacy and skills. By embedding AI education within the curriculum at an early age, we can cultivate a generation that is not only conversant with AI but also capable of contributing to its ethical and innovative application.
- **Regulatory Frameworks**: Regulations mandating the ethical deployment of AI across all sectors are essential. These regulations should ensure that AI technologies benefit society and safeguard against practices that might deepen social divides.

Integrating Generative AI into our socioeconomic systems is complex and marked by promise and perils. As we navigate this terrain, the imperative to create a milieu where the dividends of AI are universally accessible becomes increasingly apparent. This requires a concerted effort from policymakers, educators, and industry leaders alike to champion initiatives that bolster innovation and equity in tandem. By doing so, we can harness the full potential of Generative AI, not merely as a catalyst for economic growth but as a cornerstone for building a more inclusive society. In this future, the measure of our success will be the technological feats we achieve and the breadth with which we share these advancements, ensuring that Generative AI acts as a lever for socio-economic upliftment and not as a wedge driving inequality.

Conclusion

Exploring the socio-economic impacts of Generative AI unveils a dynamic interplay of challenges and opportunities reshaping our world. This technology is revolutionizing human resources, transforming how we educate and learn, and posing new social equity and access questions. The profound influence of Generative AI stretches across every facet of society, promising unparalleled economic efficiency and innovation while also highlighting the need for inclusivity and social well-being. As we forge ahead, it becomes imperative to harness Generative AI as a dual-force engine: one that drives economic prosperity and another that champions social equity. The potential of this technology to automate and innovate opens up a wealth of opportunities for growth and development. Yet, the accurate measure of progress lies in our ability to distribute these benefits equitably, ensuring that Generative AI is a bridge rather than a barrier to social advancement. Building a future where technology underpins economic growth and social progress demands a concerted effort to share the gains of AI across the entire spectrum of society.

Reflecting on the discussions in this chapter, it becomes evident that while Generative AI presents vast opportunities, it also requires careful management to ensure its benefits are equitably shared and its challenges effectively addressed. As we transition to the subsequent chapters, we will explore other dimensions of AI's impact, focusing on global trends, regulatory developments, and the future of AI integration in various sectors. This ongoing exploration is essential for developing a comprehensive understanding of the potential and the pitfalls of Generative AI, guiding us towards responsible and beneficial use of this groundbreaking technology.

9. GETTING STARTED WITH GENERATIVE AI TOOLS

Quickly ramp up on the current state of generative AI, including how to get better results from tools like ChatGPT, Anthropic Claude, and Google Bard.[1]

— SIMON ALLARDICE

This quote effectively introduces the need for solid foundational knowledge in navigating generative AI tools. In this chapter, you can explore how beginners can leverage these insights to choose the right platforms and tools, ensuring they align with their needs and objectives. Allardice's emphasis on the pragmatic introduction to generative AI is a perfect transition to discuss the practical applications and initial steps one should take when venturing into this technology.

Imagine stepping into a vast library, each book offering insights into different aspects of Generative AI. Just as a librarian would guide you

---

1. https://www.pluralsight.com/courses/generative-ai-foundations-getting-started

to the correct section based on your interests and needs, this chapter aims to help you navigate the expansive world of Generative AI tools. Whether you want to enhance your business, dive into creative projects, or explore AI out of curiosity, selecting the right tools is your first crucial step. Here, you'll discover how to assess your needs, understand the spectrum of available tools, and make informed decisions about which resources will best serve your objectives.

SELECTING THE RIGHT GENERATIVE AI TOOLS FOR YOU

Evaluating Your Needs

Your adventure into the world of Generative AI begins with a clear understanding of what you hope to achieve. Are you looking to automate tasks, generate new content, or analyze large datasets? Your objectives will influence the type of AI tools most suitable for you. For instance, a small business owner looking to understand customer sentiments might benefit from a different set of tools than a graphic designer interested in creating AI-generated art. It's essential to outline your goals clearly and consider how AI can realistically help you achieve them. This initial assessment narrows your options and sets a clear path forward, ensuring your chosen tools align perfectly with your needs.

Overview of Tools

Generative AI tools are diverse, each designed with specific capabilities and user scenarios in mind. Platforms that require minimal coding are particularly appealing for those new to AI. Tools like **RunwayML**

offer user-friendly interfaces for creative projects, allowing users to generate images, videos, and models without extensive technical knowledge. For text-based AI, platforms like ChatGPT provide intuitive ways to interact with AI to generate written content or provide coding assistance. Understanding these platforms' strengths and ideal use cases will help you select the tool that best fits your project's demands. It's about finding the correct key for the lock, ensuring that the tool does what you need it to do, complementing your skill level, and enhancing your workflow.

Datasets and APIs for AI Projects

The fuel for any Generative AI tool is data. Finding suitable datasets and knowing how to use them effectively can impact the success of your AI projects. Public datasets like those available on **Kaggle**

or **Google Dataset Search**

can provide information across various domains. Additionally, APIs like OpenAI's API allow you to tap into powerful AI models with simple programming interfaces. These resources are pivotal in teaching your AI tools to perform tasks specific to your needs. However, it's crucial to understand the quality and structure of the data you're using, as this can significantly influence the learning outcomes of your AI model.

Free vs. Paid Options

There are free and paid tools. Free tools often provide a valuable entry point, allowing you to experiment and learn without financial commitment. However, these versions may have features and usage caps limitations or need more support, often available with paid subscriptions. Premium tools, while requiring an investment, offer more robust features, greater scalability, and professional support. Deciding between these options depends on your project's complexity, your budget, and how critical the AI tool is to your core operations. For most beginners, starting with free versions or trial periods is advisable to understand the tool's utility before committing financially.

Ease of Use

For those new to AI, ease of use is paramount. User-friendly interfaces that simplify complex processes enable you to harness AI's power without becoming an expert in the underlying technology. Tools that offer drag-and-drop functionalities, pre-built templates, or interactive tutorials can be particularly beneficial. They make the learning curve less steep and ensure you can see the benefits of AI integration more quickly. This accessibility is crucial in democratizing AI technology, making it a practical option for individuals and businesses of all sizes and backgrounds.

Navigating the world of Generative AI tools is akin to setting the foundations of a house. These tools' quality, suitability, and alignment with your goals will determine the stability and functionality of all your AI endeavors. As you move forward, remember that the choice of tools is about their capabilities and how they fit into your broader objectives and workflows.

Setting Up Your First Generative AI Project

Embarking on your first Generative AI project can feel like navigating a new city without a map, exciting yet slightly overwhelming. Here, you'll discover a structured approach to initiating your AI adventure, ensuring that your first project is a valuable learning experience and sets a solid foundation for future endeavors. This guide will walk you through the crucial steps of project planning, resource gathering, tool setup, and conducting your first experiment quickly and confidently.

Project Planning

The initial planning phase is essential as it lays the groundwork for your project. Start by defining clear, achievable goals. What do you hope to accomplish with this project? Are you looking to understand consumer behavior, generate creative content, or solve a specific problem? Once your goals are set, define the project's scope—determine what success looks like and establish realistic boundaries and milestones. For instance, if your goal is to create a chatbot, define its functionalities, like answering FAQs or providing customer support, and set milestones for different phases of development, such as training the model and implementing user feedback loops. This structured planning helps maintain focus and provides a clear roadmap to follow, reducing the likelihood of project sprawl or deviations that could dilute the effectiveness of your efforts.

Resource Gathering

The next step involves gathering the necessary resources and exceptionally high-quality data, which is the lifeblood of any AI project. The quality and relevance of the data you use will directly influence the performance and reliability of your AI model. For example, if you're building a recommendation system, you'll need access to extensive data about user preferences and behaviors. Sources could include transaction histories, user ratings, or online engagement metrics. Ensure the data is diverse and representative of the user base to avoid biases in the recommendations. If such data isn't readily available, consider using synthetic data or exploring partnerships with organizations that can provide the necessary datasets. Remember, the goal is to train your AI model with accurate, comprehensive data to ensure its effectiveness in real-world applications.

Tool Setup

Once your objectives are clear and resources are in place, setting up your Generative AI tool is the next crucial step. This process involves selecting the right platform based on the earlier evaluation of your needs and the tool's capabilities. For beginners, platforms that offer intuitive, user-friendly interfaces and require minimal coding are ideal. Begin by installing the necessary software, ranging from a full-suite AI platform to specific APIs that integrate with your existing systems. During setup, pay close attention to the configuration settings, including parameters like learning rates, data input formats, and model output specifications. Each setting can significantly impact the performance of your AI tool, so it's advisable to start with recommended configurations from tool documentation or tutorials, which are often designed for general use cases.

First Experiment

Now, with your AI tool set up, it's time to launch your first experiment. This initial project should be simple but designed better to understand the tool's functionalities and potential output. For instance, if you've set up a next-generation model, you might experiment with creating blog post drafts on specific topics. Input a few prompts related to your chosen topics and analyze the AI-generated texts regarding relevance, coherence, and engagement. This experiment isn't just about testing the tool's capabilities—it's also about refining your understanding of how to interact effectively with the AI. Evaluate the results against your objectives and consider prompts or settings adjustments to align the outputs with your goals. This hands-on experience is invaluable as it not only familiarizes you with the AI tool but also enhances your ability to harness its capabilities for more complex projects in the future.

By methodically planning, gathering the right resources, setting up your tools correctly, and conducting thoughtful experiments, you are setting the stage for successfully integrating Generative AI into your work or creative endeavors. Each step, from conception to execution, builds your confidence and competence in navigating this dynamic field, paving the way for more advanced applications and innovations that could transform your approach to problems and projects in your field.

TROUBLESHOOTING COMMON GENERATIVE AI PROJECT CHALLENGES

Generative AI projects can sometimes feel like steering a ship through uncharted waters. Even with a solid plan and the right tools, you will likely encounter challenges that can impede your progress. Understanding these common pitfalls and knowing how to address them effectively is crucial in maintaining the momentum of your AI projects and achieving the desired outcomes. This section examines the typical hurdles you might face as a beginner, along with strategic advice on troubleshooting, seeking help, and fostering a culture of iterative improvement.

Common Pitfalls

Data-related issues are among the first and most frequent challenges encountered in Generative AI projects. These can range from insufficient data quantity to poor data quality, including biases or incorrect data labeling, which can severely compromise the training of your AI model. Another common issue is underestimating the complexity of the model needed. This can lead to oversimplifying the problem, thus needing to capture more nuances or overfitting, where the model is too closely fitted to the training dataset and performs poorly on new, unseen datasets. Additionally, beginners often need help with configuring the AI model correctly, which can lead to inefficient learning paths and suboptimal performance.

Debugging Tips

For data-related issues, the first step is always to perform a thorough audit of your datasets. Ensure the data is abundant, diverse, and representative of your model's real-world scenario. Tools like data visualization software can help you spot inconsistencies, biases, or anomalies in your datasets. If data quality is an issue, consider techniques like data augmentation or synthetic data generation to enhance your dataset. For model complexity and configuration challenges, it's beneficial to start with simpler models to establish baseline performance and then gradually scale up in complexity. Cross-validation techniques can help you understand how your model performs on unseen data, guiding you in simplifying or complexifying your model.

Seeking Help

Turning to the community can be an invaluable strategy when faced with persistent issues you cannot resolve alone. Numerous online forums and communities, such as **Stack Overflow**

, GitHub

, or even specific forums like the **TensorFlow**

or **PyTorch communities**

offer a wealth of knowledge and are often willing to help troubleshoot issues. Don't hesitate to post your questions there, but ensure you provide a detailed account of the problem, including what you have tried so far. This will increase your chances of receiving helpful advice. Additionally, if you use a commercial AI platform or tool, leveraging their official support channels can provide expert guidance tailored to their specific technology.

Iterative Improvement

Finally, the concept of iterative improvement is fundamental in AI. This approach is about continuously learning from each project, refining your processes, and enhancing your models with each iteration. It involves regularly reviewing the performance of your AI models, gathering feedback, and making informed adjustments. This cycle of planning, executing, reviewing, and refining improves the accuracy and efficiency of your AI solutions and deepens your understanding of the tools and the underlying principles of AI. Embrace failures and challenges as learning opportunities, and document your lessons learned to streamline future projects.

By recognizing and understanding these common pitfalls, applying practical debugging strategies, seeking help when needed, and committing to continuous improvement, you are well-equipped to navigate the complexities of Generative AI projects. This proactive and informed approach will enhance your projects' success rate and contribute to your growth and confidence as an AI practitioner.

MASTERING THE ART OF PROMPTING IN GENERATIVE AI

Prompting in the context of Generative AI refers to feeding a model with initial input or instructions that it uses as a basis to generate output. This input is crucial because it guides the AI's response, shaping its output's content and style. Therefore, crafting effective prompts is central to leveraging Generative AI tools efficiently, especially in fields requiring nuanced language, tone, and content adaptation. Whether you're a marketer seeking to generate engaging content or a developer aiming to create dynamic code, understanding how to communicate with your AI tool through prompts effectively can dramatically enhance its outputs' utility and relevance.

Discussing the types of prompts, we see a range from open-ended to specific and creative to analytical. Open-ended prompts allow the AI more creative freedom, often resulting in broader and more varied outputs. For instance, asking an AI to "write a blog post about current AI trends" is open-ended, providing room for creative interpretation. In contrast, specific prompts tightly control the AI's output by giving detailed instructions—e.g., "write a 300-word blog post summarizing the use of AI in healthcare as reported in the latest issue of the AI Journal." Here, the specificity narrows the AI, often leading to more predictable and targeted content. The choice between open-ended and specific prompts should align with your project goals and the degree of creativity or precision you need in the output.

Crafting effective prompts is an art that involves a nuanced understanding of the AI's capabilities and limitations. An effective prompt should be clear, focused, and aligned with the data on which the AI was trained. For example, a good prompt for a creative project might be, "Create a short story about a reunion between long-lost friends that takes place in a futuristic world." This prompt provides a scenario with enough detail to guide the AI but leaves room for creative embellishment. A poor prompt, on the other hand, might be too vague or too broad, such as "write something interesting," which could lead to an irrelevant or unfocused output.

Prompt engineering has emerged as a crucial area in professional and creative settings, where the ability to fine-tune prompts can determine the success of AI applications. Prompt engineering involves the strategic design of input commands to optimize the performance of AI models in generating valuable and relevant output. This practice is critical in fields such as journalism, where the tone and style of writing are crucial, or in software development, where precision in generated code is paramount.

Refining prompts often involves a process of trial and error. Initial outputs from AI might not perfectly match your expectations, necessitating prompt adjustments. This iterative process involves tweaking the wording, adding context, or specifying constraints to steer the AI towards the desired output gradually. Tools that facilitate this refinement process can include user interfaces that suggest modifications to prompts based on past outputs or provide real-time previews of generated content.

For those seeking to master the art of prompting, numerous tools and resources are available to enhance your skills. Platforms like OpenAI's GPT-3 Playground offer environments where you can experiment with different prompts and immediately see how changes affect the output. Additionally, resources like the Prompt Engineering Wiki provide guidelines and best practices shared by the community. Practical exercises, such as attempting to generate different styles of writing from the same prompt or modifying prompts to change the tone of an article, can be invaluable in honing your prompting skills.

Finally, to give you a practical edge, here are ten effective prompts designed for various AI applications and their expected outputs:

1. *Creative Writing*: "Compose a short story set in a dystopian future where AI governs society. The protagonist, a human rebel, discovers a hidden flaw in the AI's code that could bring about its downfall. Describe the

setting, characters, and pivotal moments of the plot in vivid detail."

2. *Programming Assistance*: "Generate a Python script that uses the OpenAI API to analyze sentiment in Twitter posts about a specific topic. The script should include authentication, data retrieval, sentiment analysis, and visualization of results."

3. *Marketing Copy*: "Create a compelling product description for a new eco-friendly smart home system. Highlight its unique features, such as energy-saving capabilities, integration with existing smart devices, and user-friendly interface, while emphasizing its positive impact on the environment."

4. *Educational Content*: "Write a detailed lesson plan for a high school biology class on genetic engineering. Include objectives, materials needed, a step-by-step guide for a hands-on activity, discussion questions, and assessment methods."

5. *Customer Service*: "Draft a professional email response to a customer dissatisfied with a recent purchase. The email should acknowledge the issue, offer a sincere apology, provide a solution (e.g., refund, replacement), and invite the customer to provide further feedback."

6. *Health and Wellness*: "Develop a weekly meal plan for a vegetarian diet that ensures balanced nutrition. Include breakfast, lunch, dinner, and snack options for each day, with detailed recipes, nutritional information, and tips for meal prep."

7. *Business Strategy*: "Write a detailed proposal for a new marketing campaign aimed at increasing brand awareness for a tech startup. Outline the target audience, key messages, advertising channels, timeline, budget, and metrics for measuring success."

8. *Travel Guide*: "Create a comprehensive travel itinerary for a two-week trip to Japan, focusing on cultural experiences and local cuisine. Include recommendations for cities to visit, must-see attractions, local restaurants, traditional activities, and tips for navigating the country."

9. *Personal Development*: "Write a motivational article on the importance of resilience in achieving personal and professional goals. Include real-life examples, practical strategies for building resilience, and an encouraging conclusion that inspires readers to persevere through challenges."

10. *Historical Analysis*: "Compose an essay analyzing the impact of the Industrial Revolution on urbanization in Europe. Discuss the social, economic, and environmental changes that occurred, supported by historical data and references to key events and figures."

Each of these prompts is tailored to elicit specific types of responses from AI, demonstrating the versatility and potential of carefully engineered prompts in various professional and creative contexts. Remember that working with AI is a conversation; after you have your output, continue the conversation and have AI update, enhance, and manipulate your prompt until it meets your expectations. I updated my prompt several times in my original request that started my AI interest, a complaint letter to an airline. I added the specific flight number, day, and frequent flyer number (see Introduction for that discussion).

As you explore the ever-changing world of Generative AI, we want to ensure you have access to an evolving list of prompts that can help you harness the full potential of these tools. We have curated and collected a **list of prompts** throughout the writing of this book, designed to spark creativity and enhance your projects. You will gain access to this ever-growing repository by scanning the QR code provided.

We intend to update and expand this list continually for your benefit. We invite you to contribute your prompts to foster a collaborative community. Join us in this collective endeavor to explore and innovate in the realm of Generative AI.

This exploration of the art of prompting in Generative AI enhances your interaction with AI tools and deepens your understanding of how subtle changes in input can significantly alter outcomes. As you move forward, carry with you the knowledge that effective communication with AI through well-crafted prompts is a powerful skill that can transform the potential of your projects.

QUIZ: ADVANCED TECHNIQUES IN GENERATIVE AI PROJECTS

As we conclude this chapter on advanced techniques in Generative AI projects, we must recap what we've learned and ensure these essential concepts are well grasped. The quiz that follows is not just a theoretical exercise but a practical tool designed to reinforce your understanding, emphasize crucial details, and offer insights that will prove invaluable in your future AI projects. By actively participating in this quiz, you will fortify your comprehension and pinpoint areas that could benefit from further study, making your time spent on this quiz a worthwhile investment in your professional development.

1. What is the primary purpose of cross-validation in AI model development?

    a) To reduce the size of the training dataset
    b) To evaluate the model's performance on unseen data
    c) To increase the training speed
    d) To simplify the model architecture

2. What is NOT a common pitfall in Generative AI projects?

    a) Insufficient data quantity
    b) Poor data quality
    c) Overfitting
    d) Excessive computational power

3. What does the term 'prompt engineering' refer to in the context of Generative AI?

    a) Designing input commands to optimize AI performance
    b) Developing new AI algorithms
    c) Enhancing hardware for AI models
    d) Simplifying data preprocessing steps

4. Why is iterative improvement significant in AI projects?

    a) It speeds up the development process
    b) It ensures continuous learning and model refinement
    c) It reduces the need for data cleaning
    d) It eliminates the need for model validation

5. True or False: Open-ended prompts are generally better for generating precise and targeted AI outputs.

6. True or False: Data augmentation can help improve the quality of your training dataset by adding synthetic data.

7. True or False: Seeking help from online AI communities is only helpful for beginners.

8. True or False: Effective, prompt engineering requires understanding the AI model's capabilities and the training data.

In this chapter, we've explored advanced techniques that can elevate your Generative AI projects to new heights of sophistication. By understanding common pitfalls, applying effective debugging strategies, harnessing the power of prompt engineering, and embracing iterative improvement, you can navigate AI's complexities with confidence and ingenuity. The knowledge you've gained here is not just theoretical; it forms a robust foundation for your ongoing exploration and innovation in the dynamic field of Generative AI. As you move forward, remember that mastering AI is a continuous adventure—each project, challenge, and success builds on the previous one, propelling you toward greater proficiency and discovery.

10. Global Perspectives on Generative AI

AI is like art; we did not know the void it would fill before it existed. Now, it's as essential as the air we breathe, transforming our world with every breath of innovation. [1]

— Maxwell T. Sterling (2024)

As the sun rises in different parts of the globe, so does the dawn of Generative AI, unveiling its potential in many forms unique to each region. This chapter invites you on a detailed adventure to uncover how diverse cultures and nations are not just participating in but actively molding the future of Generative AI. It's like how local ingredients and distinct regional flavors add depth and variety to worldwide cuisine. Similarly, each nation's unique characteristics and cultural insights contribute to the growth and development of Generative AI. This global collaboration results in a vibrant

---

1. This author in this book, right now. ChatGPT enhanced my original quotation and Grammarly also provided counsel and verified that it was indeed an original quotation.

mosaic of innovation, where the contributions of each culture extend the boundaries of what's possible, weaving a complex narrative that is as varied as humanity itself. Through this exploration, we'll see how global Generative AI is not just shaped by technology but is deeply influenced by human creativity and cultural heritage, offering a panoramic view of its integration into the fabric of our lives.

GENERATIVE AI INNOVATIONS AROUND THE WORLD

Global Innovation Ecosystems

Around the globe, countries are cultivating distinctive innovation ecosystems that significantly influence the development and application of Generative AI. These ecosystems, comprising universities, tech startups, established corporations, and government policies, create a fertile ground for AI research and innovation. In Silicon Valley, the synergy between academic institutions like Stanford University and technology giants such as Google and Apple fosters an environment where theoretical AI research rapidly transitions into practical, market-leading applications. Contrastingly, in Israel, a focus on cybersecurity and defense technologies fuels AI advancements, supported by robust government backing and compulsory military service that often includes advanced tech training. Each ecosystem's unique set of resources, priorities, and talents contributes differently but significantly to global AI, ensuring multiple approaches and solutions.

Cultural Influence on AI Development

Cultural factors profoundly influence the direction and nature of AI research and development, leading to a diversity in application that reflects regional needs and values. For example, Japan's aging population has steered its AI focus towards robotics that can assist elderly citizens, blending Japan's cultural respect for older people with its prowess in robotics and technology. In contrast, India's vast linguistic diversity has prompted local AI research to focus on natural language processing to break down language barriers and enable more inclusive communication and technology access. These cultural underpinnings ensure that AI development is not a monolith but a mosaic, rich with variability and tuned to local contexts.

International Collaboration

Collaborations across borders highlight the universal language of innovation that Generative AI speaks. One notable collaboration is the partnership between European countries in the Human Brain Project,

which aims to advance neuroscience, computing, and brain-related medicine through AI. This project accelerates understanding of the human brain and pioneers new ways AI can be modeled on human neural structures. Another example of international collaboration is the partnership between U.S. and Chinese researchers focusing on AI-driven environmental protection projects, illustrating how joint efforts can address global challenges like climate change.

Emerging Leaders in AI

Emerging leaders in Generative AI are open to more than just the traditional powerhouses of the U.S. and China. Countries like Sweden and Canada are making significant advances driven by solid academic institutions, supportive government policies, and ethical frameworks for AI. Sweden's commitment to sustainability has propelled it to lead in AI applications focused on energy efficiency and environmental data analysis. Meanwhile, Canada's early investment in AI education and research, exemplified by institutions like the Vector Institute, continues to yield a cadre of AI talent and startups focused on healthcare and ecological technologies. These regions demonstrate that leadership in AI innovation can emerge from a commitment to nurturing talent, supporting research and development, and aligning technological advances with national priorities and values.

As Generative AI continues to evolve, the contributions from various parts of the world ensure its development is robust, innovative, and reflective of our diverse global village. This diversity is crucial, as it brings different perspectives and solutions to the table, ensuring that AI technologies evolve in a way that is inclusive and beneficial to all. As we continue to explore these global perspectives, remember that each contribution, no matter how small or localized, plays a part in shaping the future of AI, making it a truly international endeavor.

CULTURAL CONSIDERATIONS IN AI DEVELOPMENT AND USE

In Generative AI, where technology meets diverse human experiences, cultural considerations play a pivotal role in shaping both the development and the adoption of AI technologies. As you explore the multifaceted interactions between culture and AI, it becomes evident that cultural biases, if unaddressed, can skew AI outcomes, leading to solutions that may not be universally applicable or fair. For instance, facial recognition technologies developed primarily with datasets comprising images of individuals from predominantly one ethnic background have shown decreased accuracy rates when identifying people from other ethnic groups. This raises concerns about fairness and discrimination and highlights the necessity for culturally diverse data to train AI systems. Ensuring that AI algorithms are exposed to a wide range of cultural contexts can mitigate these biases, making these systems more inclusive and effective across diverse global populations.

Language and localization present significant challenges in developing Generative AI that serves a global audience. The complexity lies not only in translating text but also in understanding and conveying the nuances that are often deeply rooted in cultural contexts. For example, idiomatic expressions and local slang, heavily influenced by cultural idiosyncrasies, can be particularly challenging for AI to process and generate accurately. Addressing these challenges involves developing AI models that are not only multilingual but also culturally aware. This can be achieved by incorporating localized datasets and employing linguists who can provide insights into the subtleties of language and communication styles specific to different cultures. Moreover, advancements in NLP are increasingly focusing on contextual understanding, which can significantly enhance the effectiveness of AI in managing language nuances, thereby improving user interactions with AI systems in diverse linguistic environments.

The potential of Generative AI to preserve and promote cultural heritage opens up exciting possibilities. Around the globe, AI is being leveraged to digitize and analyze historical documents, artifacts, and artworks, making them more accessible and preserving them for future generations. In language preservation, AI tools are being developed to document and revive endangered languages by creating digital resources for language learning and usage. For instance, AI-driven projects are underway that involve the collection of spoken and written samples of lesser-known languages, which are then used to train AI models. These models can generate new content in these languages, providing a vital resource for educational and cultural preservation efforts. Similarly, AI is being used to analyze and replicate traditional crafts and art forms in the arts, offering new ways to engage with and sustain cultural expressions that might otherwise be at risk of fading into obscurity.

Ethical and social norms significantly influence how Generative AI technologies are received and integrated into daily life across different societies. In some cultures, there may be a higher degree of skepticism or ethical concern regarding AI due to prevailing religious or philosophical beliefs about the nature of intelligence and the role of machines in society. In others, there might be a more enthusiastic acceptance of AI technologies driven by a cultural emphasis on innovation and technological advancement. Understanding these cultural dynamics is crucial for AI developers navigating the complex terrain of global AI deployment. It requires a sensitive approach that respects and adheres to local ethical standards and social norms, ensuring that AI solutions are technologically sound and culturally consonant. Engaging with local communities, policymakers, and cultural experts can provide valuable insights that guide the development of AI applications, ensuring they resonate well with local populations while adhering to ethical standards that uphold dignity, privacy, and fairness.

As you explore the cultural dimensions of AI, it becomes clear that the path to genuinely global and fair AI solutions lies in embracing and integrating human cultures into the fabric of AI development. This approach enriches the technology and ensures its relevance and sustainability in a world of incredible cultural diversity and complexity.

INTERNATIONAL AI INITIATIVES AND COLLABORATIONS

As Generative AI continues to redefine the edges of what technology can achieve, the role of international cooperation has become ever more critical. Nations around the globe are not only collaborating but also engaging in a healthy competition that propels the field forward at an extraordinary pace. This synergy of cooperative efforts and competitive spirit is shaping the trajectory of AI development, ensuring that advancements in AI are both rapid and responsibly guided by shared human-centric values.

In recent years, significant international initiatives have been launched to foster collaboration on AI development while aligning with ethical standards. One of the most notable is the Global Partnership on Artificial Intelligence ("GPAI")

This international consortium includes Canada, France, Germany, Italy, Japan, the United Kingdom, the United States, and the European Union. This partnership focuses on ensuring that AI development is steered towards enhancing the quality of life globally, respecting human rights, and promoting the responsible use of AI. GPAI is a forum for sharing best practices and research findings, which helps harmonize approaches to AI governance and develop-ment across different countries. By fostering dialogue among nations,

GPAI aims to preempt the fragmentation of ethical standards and ensure that AI technologies are developed globally with beneficial and fair intent.

Another AI collaboration is the AI4EU platform,

which exemplifies how European countries pool their resources and expertise to create a cohesive AI ecosystem. This initiative is designed to make AI tools and resources widely accessible, promoting innovation and facilitating the integration of AI into various sectors of the economy and society. AI4EU supports research and development and addresses societal challenges such as healthcare, climate science, and media integrity. By creating a centralized platform, AI4EU enables researchers, developers, and businesses to collaborate more effectively, accelerating the pace of AI innovation in Europe while ensuring it aligns with broader social values and regulatory frameworks.

While collaboration fosters shared growth and learning, competition in AI development catalyzes rapid technological advancements. For instance, China's New Generation Artificial Intelligence Development Plan

has set ambitious goals to become the world leader in AI by 2030. This plan is about advancing Chinese technology and integrating AI into the economy, education, and the military, thereby transforming the societal fabric. Similarly, the United States National AI Initiative

aims to ensure continued leadership in AI by doubling research and development, enhancing the AI workforce, and leading international engagement in AI. These competitive national strategies drive technological innovation at an unparalleled speed, pushing each nation to invest in and significantly advance the field of AI.

The impact of these international collaborations and competitions on AI development is profound. They accelerate technological innovation and ensure a broader dissemination of benefits. By sharing knowledge, resources, and ethical frameworks, countries can leverage AI to address global challenges more effectively, from pandemics and climate change to economic inequality and international security.

These efforts underscore the potential of AI as a transformative force for good, provided it is guided by a commitment to enhancing human welfare and upholding ethical standards.

This diversity in ethical perspectives necessitates international cooperation to address AI ethics effectively. One pivotal example of such efforts is **UNESCO's Recommendation on the Ethics of Artificial Intelligence, adopted in November 2022.**

This landmark document provides a global standard for AI ethics, emphasizing fairness, accountability, and transparency. It marks a significant step towards establishing universally agreed-upon principles that guide AI development and use, aiming to foster innovations that respect human rights and promote social welfare.

International AI initiatives and collaborations are likely to evolve further. As AI technologies become increasingly embedded in every aspect of human life, the need for global cooperation in managing these technologies becomes more acute. Balancing competition and collaboration will be crucial in fostering an environment where AI advances national interests and contributes to worldwide welfare and security. The ongoing dialogues and partnerships will be pivotal in shaping a future where AI technologies are developed responsibly and beneficially, reflecting the global community's collective aspirations and ethical standards.

As this chapter concludes, we reflect on the dynamic interplay of collaboration and competition in the international AI arena. This intricate dance not only drives technological advancements but also ensures these advancements are grounded in ethical practices and aimed at improving the human condition globally. We now turn our attention to the subsequent chapter, which will explore the regulatory frameworks that govern AI development and how laws and policies adapt to the challenges posed by these rapidly evolving technologies. This exploration will be crucial in understanding how governance can keep pace with innovation, ensuring AI's benefits are maximized while its risks are minimized.

11. Navigating the Complexities of AI Ethics

Artificial intelligence does not merely extend the power and potential of human intellect, it also magnifies our ongoing ethical responsibilities[1]

— SHANNON VALLOR

As twilight settles over the horizon of modern technology, the shadows cast by the burgeoning capabilities of artificial intelligence grow longer and more intricate. Among these shadows, ethical dilemmas present scenarios that challenge our understanding and management of AI's impact on society. Like a lantern, this chapter aims to illuminate the path by exploring real-world case studies where AI ethics were tested. Through these explorations, you will gain insights into the ethical quandaries that AI can present, learn from the responses crafted by those at the helm, and consider how these lessons can shape a more ethically aware AI.

---

1. Vallor, S. (2016). *Technology and the virtues: A philosophical guide to a future worth wanting.* Oxford University Press.

CASE STUDIES IN AI ETHICS: LEARNING FROM REAL-WORLD SCENARIOS

The Autonomous Vehicles Dilemma

One of the most publicized ethical challenges in AI comes from the automotive industry, particularly concerning autonomous vehicles ("AV"s). Consider a scenario where an AV must choose between two dire outcomes: colliding with a pedestrian or swerving and risking the lives of its passengers. This real-world dilemma, known as the "trolley problem," has been at the forefront of discussions about programming ethics in AI. Companies like Tesla and Waymo have faced these challenges head-on, navigating complex decisions about whose safety is prioritized in unavoidable crash scenarios. The outcomes of these situations have led to a broader understanding of the need for transparent, ethical guidelines in programming AVs and have spurred public debates about the moral frameworks that should guide AI decision-making.

AI in Recruitment: Bias and Fairness

Another sector where AI ethics have been rigorously tested is human resources, particularly in AI-driven recruitment processes. Amazon's scrapped AI recruiting tool serves as a cautionary tale; it inadvertently learned to favor male candidates over females due to biases in the training data—historic job applications dominated by men. This case underscores the critical importance of unbiased data in training AI systems and highlights the need for ongoing monitoring to prevent AI from perpetuating existing inequalities. It also serves as a vital lesson in the potential consequences of unchecked AI, guiding future AI applications towards more ethical and fair practices.

Healthcare AI: Privacy and Consent

The healthcare sector has also been a fertile ground for ethical AI applications, especially concerning patient data privacy and consent. A notable instance involved Google's DeepMind and the UK's National Health Service, where the use of patient data to test a new app raised concerns about the legality and ethics of patient consent. This partnership faced scrutiny and criticism, leading to a reassessment of how patient data is handled and emphasizing the need for absolute transparency and strict adherence to privacy regulations in healthcare collaborations involving AI.

Diverse Perspectives from Around the Globe

These case studies highlight the ethical challenges specific to different sectors and underscore the varied cultural and regulatory responses to these challenges. The European Union's General Data Protection Regulation provides a stringent framework that impacts how companies worldwide handle data privacy, influencing global AI practices. Meanwhile, in Asian markets, where regulatory frameworks might differ, the emphasis might be placed more on the collective good than individual privacy.

Visual Element: Ethical Decision-Making Flowchart

To help you understand and navigate these complex scenarios, consider this visual element—a flowchart that outlines a step-by-step decision-making process in ethical dilemmas. This tool lets you visualize the paths that can be taken when confronted with a moral decision in AI, emphasizing the importance of considering multiple perspectives and consequences before concluding.

This chapter dissects these real-world applications and their ripple effects across various industries and communities. It does not merely recount tales of caution but serves as a primer on the necessity for a proactive and profoundly ethical approach to AI development and deployment. As AI integrates more into daily life, the lessons drawn from these experiences are invaluable in guiding not just current but future applications of AI, ensuring that they are aligned with ethical standards and human values.

DEVELOPING A PERSONAL ETHICAL FRAMEWORK FOR AI USE

In the burgeoning field of artificial intelligence, where the pace of innovation frequently outstrips the development of corresponding ethical guidelines, it becomes imperative for individuals and organizations alike to establish a robust ethical framework. Such a framework serves as a compass to navigate the complex ethics of AI and as a foundational pillar supporting the responsible evolution of AI technologies. Let's explore how you can develop and apply your ethical framework, ensuring your engagement with AI remains aligned with your core values and principles.

Identifying Core Values

The first step in creating an ethical framework for AI use is to identify and clearly define your core values. These values are the bedrock upon which all further ethical considerations and decisions rest. For instance, if transparency and accountability are central to your values, these should be reflected in how you choose, design, and deploy AI solutions. Begin by listing values you hold in high regard, such as fairness, privacy, or benevolence, and consider how AI might impact these. It's crucial to thoroughly examine how these values intersect with AI's capabilities and limitations. For example, consider an AI system designed for recruitment; aligning this system with a value like fairness would require mechanisms to mitigate any biases in the AI's decision-making processes actively.

Framework Creation

Once your core values are established, the next step is to translate these values into a structured ethical framework. This framework should offer clear guidelines for implementing these values in practical AI scenarios. Creating this framework involves defining specific ethical standards, practices, or policies that will guide the development and use of AI technologies. For example, if one of your core values is respect for user privacy, your framework might include standards for data encryption, anonymization techniques, and strict data access controls. Furthermore, this framework should address the broader impact of AI applications, considering potential long-term effects on societal norms and individual behaviors. Developing such a framework requires a deep understanding of ethical principles and an informed awareness of AI's technological aspects and broader societal implications.

Applying the Framework

With a framework in place, the focus shifts to its application across various AI-related activities and decisions. This application acts as both a test and a demonstration of the framework's effectiveness in real-world scenarios. For instance, if your framework prioritizes non-maleficence, applying this principle might involve conducting rigorous impact assessments before deploying AI systems to identify and mitigate potential harm. Consider a scenario where you're implementing an AI-driven health diagnostic tool; applying your ethical framework would necessitate a thorough validation of the AI's diagnostic accuracy and reliability across diverse populations to prevent harmful outcomes due to errors or biases. This stage is critical for refining the framework, as it highlights areas where theoretical ethical commitments meet practical challenges, requiring adjustments or enhancements to ensure the framework remains relevant and robust.

Let's put your knowledge to the test! Below is a quiz designed to help you reflect on the ethical considerations and frameworks discussed in the chapter. Your responses will give insight into how well you have grasped the key concepts and how you might apply these ethical principles in real-world AI scenarios.

Quiz

1. What is the first step in creating an ethical framework for AI use?

   a. Identify potential risks and benefits of AI technology.
   b. Develop a list of AI applications in various industries.
   c. Identify and define your core values.
   d. Create a policy document for AI governance.

2. Which value is crucial when designing AI systems to ensure fairness in AI-driven decisions?

    a. Efficiency
    b. Transparency
    c. Scalability
    d. Cost-effectiveness

3. In the context of AI ethics, what does the application of a framework involve?

    a. Strictly following the government regulations without modification.
    b. Testing the framework in theoretical scenarios only.
    c. Applying the framework to real-world scenarios and making necessary adjustments.
    d. Using the framework to guide the technological development of AI systems only.

4. How should ethical frameworks in AI evolve?

    a. They should remain static to maintain consistency.
    b. They should be adapted based on technological changes and societal needs.
    c. They should focus exclusively on new AI technologies.
    d. They should be simplified as AI technology becomes more complex.

5. What role does transparency play in the ethical use of AI in recruitment processes?

    a. It is unrelated to ethical considerations.
    b. It ensures that all stakeholders understand the decision-making process.
    c. It minimizes the cost of implementing AI.
    d. It speeds up the recruitment process.

Reflecting on your quiz answers, consider how these ethical principles can be integrated into your ongoing engagement with AI, ensuring that your practices align with your values and the broader societal expectations.

Answer Key:

1. c. Identifying and defining your core values.
2. b. Transparency
3. c. Applying the framework to real-world scenarios and making necessary adjustments.
4. b. They should be adapted based on technological changes and societal needs.
5. b. It ensures that all stakeholders understand the decision-making process.

Adaptation and Evolution

Finally, an ethical framework for AI is not a static entity but a dynamic one that requires continuous evaluation and adaptation. As AI technology evolves and new ethical challenges emerge, your framework must evolve to address these changes effectively. This adaptation might involve incorporating new ethical insights from ongoing AI research, revising policies in response to emerging AI applications, or recalibrating ethical priorities considering shifting societal values. For example, advancements in AI capabilities like deep learning might raise new privacy concerns that were not previously considered, necessitating updates to your framework to address these issues adequately. Moreover, the global conversation on AI ethics continues to evolve, often leading to new consensus or regulatory changes that your framework must accommodate to stay current and effective.

By systematically identifying your core values, creating a structured ethical framework, applying it across real-world scenarios, and continuously adapting it, you ensure that your AI engagement is ethically sound and socially responsible. This approach fosters trust and credibility in your AI endeavors and contributes to the broader goal of steering AI development toward beneficial and sustainable outcomes.

The Global Conversation on AI Ethics and Regulation

As artificial intelligence weaves its threads more profoundly into the societal fabric, the tapestry of global perspectives on AI ethics becomes increasingly intricate and diversified. Around the world, nations grapple with the dual challenge of harnessing AI's potential while mitigating its risks, leading to a rich dialogue that shapes the evolving AI ethics. This dialogue is not confined within the borders of any single country; it is a robust exchange of ideas, concerns, and visions that transcends geographical and cultural boundaries.

The ethical perspectives on AI vary significantly across regions, influenced by cultural values, historical experiences, and socio-economic priorities. For instance, European approaches often emphasize individual rights and data privacy, as seen in the stringent GDPR. This regulation has set a global benchmark for data privacy, influencing how AI systems that process the personal data of EU citizens are designed, regardless of where the AI company is based. In contrast, countries like China prioritize state security and technological supremacy, leading to different regulatory emphases that impact AI development and deployment. Meanwhile, nations such as Japan integrate societal harmony and the integration of technology into everyday life, fostering public trust and further AI acceptance.

The regulatory environment for AI is complex and continuously evolving. In addition to broad ethical guidelines, specific regulations are being proposed and implemented to address the nuanced challenges posed by AI. For example, updates to the GDPR are being considered to tackle the unique risks associated with AI, such as deep learning algorithms that can make decisions that are challenging to interpret. These updates focus on enhancing transparency and ensuring that AI systems can be audited for compliance with data protection laws. By aligning AI development with these standards, nations safeguard individual rights and enhance the reliability and trustworthiness of AI applications across various sectors.

The roles of various stakeholders—governments, corporations, and civil society—are critical in shaping AI ethics. Governments are tasked with creating and enforcing regulations that balance innovation with ethical considerations. Corporations, particularly those driving AI advancements, must adhere to these regulations while actively engaging in ethical self-regulation, often going beyond compliance to establish best practices. Civil society, including academic institutions, non-governmental organizations, and the general public, plays a watchdog role. It also provides a platform for raising ethical concerns and pushing for more stringent or comprehensive regulatory measures.

Looking towards the future, the field of AI ethics is set to encounter rapid changes, mirroring the pace of AI technology itself. Speculative trends suggest an increase in the sophistication of AI systems, necessitating even more robust ethical frameworks and regulatory measures. Issues like AI consciousness and autonomous decision-making will likely come to the forefront, challenging existing ethical paradigms and pushing for innovative responses. Moreover, as AI becomes more integrated into critical infrastructure and essential services, ensuring these systems are ethically aligned and regulated will become even more imperative.

As we conclude this exploration of the global dialogue on AI ethics and regulation, while the challenges are daunting, the collaborative efforts underway provide a foundation for optimism. By continuing to foster international dialogue and cooperation, adapting rules to keep pace with technological advancements, and ensuring all voices are heard in the conversation, we can steer AI development towards outcomes that are not only innovative but also inclusive, fair, and ethically sound. This chapter sets the stage for the following discussions on practical implementations of these ethical real-world AI applications, ensuring that the theoretical principles explored here are translated into concrete actions that benefit society.

As this chapter closes, it draws a comprehensive picture of the dynamic interplay between innovation and regulation in AI. The emerging trends highlight a move towards greater accountability and transparency, international cooperation underscores the global nature of technological challenges, and the future points towards an increasingly complex regulatory environment that seeks to balance innovation with public good. The discussions and developments in AI regulation shape the technologies and reflect our societal values and priorities—they are a testament to our collective endeavor to steer the course of technological evolution in directions that enhance and enrich human life.

As we turn the page, the narrative shifts from the frameworks governing AI to exploring your inclusion in the community and how you keep up to date on the ever-changing field of AI.

12. COMMUNITY AND COLLABORATION AND KEEPING UP-TO-DATE

In technology, learning is not a one-time event but a continuous journey. Every day offers a new piece of knowledge and the opportunity to apply it creatively.[1]

— SUDAR PICHAI

Artificial intelligence is both a beacon and a challenge in the vast expanses of the digital age, where algorithms whisper secrets of a new era and data flows like rivers feeding civilizations. Imagine yourself not just navigating this transformation but shaping it, your voice melding into the chorus of innovation that defines the future of AI. This chapter illuminates the path to finding your tribe within the AI community, a network of minds connected by curiosity and driven by the quest for knowledge.

---

1. Pichai, S. (2022). *The importance of lifelong learning in technology.* Retrieved from https://www.wired.com

FINDING YOUR TRIBE: AI COMMUNITIES AND HOW TO ENGAGE

Discovering AI Communities

In your exploration through the world of AI, discovering communities that resonate with your interests and level of expertise is akin to finding an oasis in a desert. These communities, from online forums and social media groups to professional organizations and academic circles, offer more than just information; they provide a sense of belonging and a shared purpose. Initiating this search might seem daunting, but start by identifying what fascinates you about AI. Whether it's the ethical implications of AI, its applications in healthcare, or the intricacies of machine learning models, there's a community out there sharing your passion.

Navigating through platforms like LinkedIn, Reddit, Facebook or even specific AI community websites can unveil worlds where discussions, webinars, and collaborative projects are at your fingertips. Engaging with these communities can transform from mere participation to a vital part of your learning and professional growth. The benefits of joining such forums are manifold—they serve as a support system, a brainstorming collective, and a news source on the latest trends and breakthroughs in AI.

Engagement Strategies

Engaging effectively in AI communities involves more than passive observation. Active participation can significantly enhance your learning experience and establish your presence in the field. Start by contributing to discussions, asking insightful questions, and sharing relevant articles or studies. This approach deepens your understanding and helps you gain visibility as a proactive member.

Respectful listening is equally crucial. AI attracts minds from diverse disciplines and cultures, each bringing unique perspectives that enrich conversations. By listening attentively, you respect your peers' expertise and viewpoints and open yourself to learning opportunities that could bypass one-dimensional thinking.

Networking Benefits

The networking opportunities within AI communities are robust. Engaging with peers and experts can lead to mentorship opportunities, collaborative projects, and career advancements. These relationships are based on shared interests, experiences, and mutual respect, often blossoming into professional collaborations that influence future AI innovations.

Building Your Presence

As you become more comfortable within these communities, consider sharing your insights and experiences. Blogging about your AI projects or presenting at community meetups can mark your transition from a community member to a thought leader. When shared, your unique adventure in AI can inspire others and contribute to the community's growth, creating a legacy of knowledge and encouragement.

Attending AI Conferences and Meetups

To immerse yourself further, attend AI conferences and meetups. These gatherings are about absorbing information and experiencing the communal energy of shared enthusiasm for AI. They provide a platform to witness groundbreaking presentations, participate in workshops, and engage in one-on-one conversations with leaders in the field. Each conference can significantly broaden your understanding and expose you to new dimensions of AI.

Online Collaboration Platforms

Platforms like **GitHub**

or collaborative AI research tools offer spaces where you can work on projects with others worldwide. These platforms facilitate the sharing of code and research papers and provide forums for discussion and feedback, making collaborative AI projects more accessible and impactful.

COLLABORATIVE AI PROJECTS: LEARNING FROM COLLECTIVE INTELLIGENCE

In the evolution of artificial intelligence, collaborative projects that blend diverse perspectives and collective intelligence are enhancing and revolutionizing the field. The power of collaboration in AI extends beyond mere pooling of resources—it fosters an environment where innovative ideas flourish, challenges are tackled more efficiently, and knowledge circulates freely among participants. When diverse minds from different backgrounds and various skill sets converge on AI projects, the creative boundaries of what can be achieved expand exponentially. This synergy accelerates the development of robust AI solutions and ensures these solutions are well-rounded and consider multiple facets of any problem.

Finding the right partners for collaborative AI projects can be pivotal. The quest begins within the AI communities you are already a part of, where you've engaged and interacted with peers who share your interests. However, expanding your search to other platforms, like specialized online forums dedicated to AI collaborations or attending hackathons, can open doors to new partnerships. These venues provide unique opportunities to connect with potential collaborators who not only share your passion for AI. However, they also bring complementary skills that enhance your project's scope and depth. Engaging in discussions, participating in community challenges, and contributing to shared community resources can increase your visibility and attract like-minded professionals equally eager to collaborate.

Successful collaboration in AI often follows models that encourage openness and shared goals. Open-source projects are quintessential examples where developers and researchers from around the globe contribute to a joint project, such as **TensorFlow**

or **Apache Mahout**.

These platforms are about coding and solving problems together, learning from each other, and pushing the boundaries of what AI can achieve. Another effective model is forming formal research partnerships, which might involve multiple organizations, including universities, tech companies, and government institutions, working together on large-scale AI initiatives. These partnerships often have clear structures and defined roles that help streamline the collaborative efforts, ensuring that every participant's contribution aligns with the overarching project goals.

Several case studies highlight the success of collaborative AI projects. One notable example is the partnership between a major tech company and an academic institution, where they collaboratively developed an AI model that significantly improves the prediction of weather patterns, benefiting agriculture and disaster management efforts globally. Another example is a community-driven AI project that created an open-source tool for diagnosing diseases through image processing. This tool has been adopted by healthcare professionals in various countries, providing low-cost diagnostic support and saving countless lives. These cases exemplify how collaborative efforts lead to technological advancements and contribute solutions to some of the world's most pressing issues.

In essence, the collaborative projects in AI harness the collective intelligence of a global community, bringing together diverse perspectives that enrich the development process. This collaboration leads to innovative solutions and cultivates a culture of shared knowledge and mutual growth, indispensable in the fast-evolving field of artificial intelligence. As these partnerships continue to grow, they underscore the transformative potential of working together in AI, highlighting that the future of AI development is not just in the hands of individuals but equally in the collaborations that bridge across borders, disciplines, and cultures.

ANNUAL UPDATE PLAN: STAYING AHEAD IN GENERATIVE AI

In Generative AI, staying updated is not merely beneficial but essential. An annual update plan can serve as your roadmap to ensure that you remain at the cutting edge of or at least keep up with AI developments and continue to grow your expertise. This structured approach allows you to systematically refresh your knowledge base and adapt to the latest advancements in the field, keeping you at the forefront of this exciting and rapidly evolving domain. Here's how you can craft an effective annual update plan:

1. Identify Key Focus Areas:

Identify the core AI areas most relevant to your career or interests. These include machine learning, neural networks, robotics, natural language processing, and ethical AI. Focusing on specific domains enables you to target your learning efforts more efficiently and stay abreast of the most pertinent innovations.

2. Subscribe to Leading Journals and Magazines:

Ensure you subscribe to leading AI journals and magazines such as:

AI Magazine

Communications of the ACM

Journal of Artificial Intelligence Research

These publications provide peer-reviewed articles, cutting-edge research findings, and expert opinions crucial for staying informed about the latest in AI.

3. Set Up Digital Alerts:

Use tools like Google Scholar alerts to receive notifications about new research in your specified areas of interest. By setting alerts for keywords such as 'Generative AI' or 'Deep Learning Applications,' you can ensure that you are immediately informed of the latest academic and practical advancements. Digital alerts are a powerful way to stay updated in real-time, ensuring you don't miss any significant developments in your chosen AI domains.

Additionally, subscribing to reputable AI-focused blogs and websites can provide a more digestible format for complex information. Websites like **Towards Data Science**

on Medium offer articles written by AI professionals and enthusiasts who often discuss current trends and practical applications of AI technologies. Similarly, **ArXiv.org**

at Cornell University hosts pre-publication research papers discussing cutting-edge AI developments before reaching academic journals.

Another practical approach is utilizing RSS feeds from respected AI research institutions like the Stanford AI Lab or OpenAI. These feeds bring the latest research summaries and updates directly to your RSS feed reader, allowing for quick reviews of recent advancements without needing active searches.

4. Plan to Attend Key Conferences:

Identify and plan to attend at least one major AI conference each year, such as the Neural Information Processing Systems Conference ("NeurIPS" or https://neurips.cc/) and the International Conference on Machine Learning ("ICML" or https://icml.cc/) or an AI symposium relevant to your specialty. [I would have added a QR Code for them, but the 2024 conference is what is listed, and with any luck, this book will be relevant long after, so google them. I have attached the links for the current conferences, however.]

These conferences are hubs for learning about the latest research, offering a unique opportunity to hear from leading experts, gain insights into emerging trends, and network with other AI professionals and thought leaders. Attending conferences can significantly contribute to your professional growth and help you stay at the forefront of AI developments.

5. Engage in the Community:

Platforms such as Reddit offer a wide array of subreddits like

r/MachineLearning,
r/Artificial,
r/DeepLearning,
r/AI,
r/DataScience,
r/ArtificialIntelligence.

each catering to different facets of AI. For more structured discussions, professional networks such as LinkedIn host numerous AI groups where industry experts share insights and advancements. Additionally, websites like **Stack Exchange**

provide a more Q&A-driven approach to community interaction, which can be particularly beneficial when seeking solutions to specific problems or needing detailed explanations of complex topics.

The benefits of engaging with these communities are manifold. Firstly, sharing and gaining knowledge in a collaborative environment expedites your learning process. More experienced members often share tutorials, research papers, and case studies that can provide deeper insights into areas you are exploring. Furthermore, community forums are ideal for crowdsourcing solutions to problems. Posting a query about a bug in your AI model or seeking advice on the best algorithms for a particular project can yield multiple perspectives and solutions, enriching your understanding and providing practical guidance.

6. Engage with Online Courses:

Platforms like Coursera, Udacity, and edX continuously update their offerings to reflect new developments in AI. Each year, select at least one course that can help expand your skills or update your knowledge of new technologies and methodologies in AI. Online courses offer the flexibility to direct your learning, access to a wide range of AI topics, and the opportunity to learn from leading experts in the field, making them an excellent addition to your annual update plan.

7. Participate in Workshops and Webinars:

Look for workshops and webinars throughout the year. These are often more specific and practical than broader conference presentations and can provide hands-on experience or more profound insights into specialized topics.

8. Review and Reflect:

Review the knowledge you've gained at the end of each year and assess how it integrates with your existing expertise. Reflect on any significant changes in the AI and consider adjusting your focus areas if necessary. This process of self-evaluation and adaptation is a powerful tool that puts you in control of your learning adventure, empowering you to stay relevant and ahead in the dynamic field of AI.

9. Document Your Learning:

Keep a record of your learning activities throughout the year. This can include summaries of articles read, critical takeaways from conferences, and certificates from courses completed. This documentation will serve as a personal knowledge database, helping you track your progress, revisit critical learnings, and identify areas for further exploration. It will also assist in showcasing your continual professional development in the field, which can be valuable for career advancement and professional networking.

10. Share Your Knowledge:

Consider sharing your knowledge through blogging, teaching, or presenting at local meetups or conferences. Teaching is a powerful method for deepening one's understanding and staying engaged with the AI community.

Following this annual update plan, you commit to a structured method of keeping your AI skills and knowledge fresh and relevant. This commitment will enable you to keep pace with AI's rapid developments and position yourself as a knowledgeable and skilled professional in this dynamic field.

FUTUREPROOFING YOUR CAREER IN THE AGE OF AI

In an era where technological advancements redefine the traditional workplace, adapting to the integration of AI becomes not just a necessity but an opportunity for career growth and innovation. The infusion of AI technologies into various sectors is transforming job roles and tasks, making it imperative for professionals to adapt to these changes to stay relevant and competitive. For instance, in industries like finance and healthcare, AI automates complex data analysis tasks, shifting professionals' focus towards interpretive, strategic roles that leverage AI outputs rather than performing the analyses themselves. Embracing AI can open up new career paths in areas such as AI strategy and policy, AI safety and ethics, and AI integration, where human oversight and strategic thinking are crucial.

Developing core competencies tailored to the AI era is essential to navigate this shift effectively. Data literacy, for example, becomes crucial as professionals must understand and interpret AI-generated data-driven insights. Similarly, a deep understanding of AI ethics is required to ensure that AI implementations are fair and do not inadvertently perpetuate biases or ethical lapses. Additionally, the ability to collaborate effectively with AI systems and teams working on AI technologies is a valuable skill. This involves understanding the capabilities and limitations of AI tools and communicating effectively with technical and non-technical stakeholders about AI projects.

Continuous education and skill enhancement are pivotal in maintaining the agility to adapt to rapid technological changes. Engaging in lifelong learning through online courses, specialized workshops, and certifications can keep your skills current. Platforms like Coursera and Udacity offer AI and machine learning courses that industry experts design to cater to varying proficiency levels and professional needs. Moreover, attending AI conferences and seminars can provide insights into the latest research and trends in the field, allowing you to anticipate and prepare for shifts in technology and industry demands.

Ethical considerations are also paramount for professionals working with AI technologies. As AI becomes more prevalent, the moral implications of its use become more complex and far-reaching. Professionals must advocate for and adhere to ethical standards in AI development and application, ensuring that AI solutions are used responsibly. This includes championing transparency in AI operations, advocating for privacy and data protection, and working to eliminate biases in AI algorithms. By upholding these ethical standards, professionals contribute to the trustworthiness and reliability of AI technologies and champion a culture of responsibility critical to AI's sustainable growth.

Navigating career transitions in an AI-driven world also involves identifying and seizing opportunities in growth sectors where AI is expected to impact significantly. Fields like AI healthcare diagnostics, AI-enhanced cybersecurity, and AI-driven environmental planning rapidly grow and require specialized knowledge and skills. Transitioning into these areas may require targeted reskilling efforts, such as acquiring specific technical skills related to AI applications in these fields or understanding the regulatory and societal implications of deploying AI in such contexts.

Finally, developing resilience in AI-driven changes involves actively participating in networks and communities focused on AI. Engaging with these communities can provide support, broaden your understanding, and offer opportunities for collaboration and innovation. It encourages a proactive approach to career development, equipping you with the insights and networks needed to thrive in a technology-driven future.

This exploration of strategies to future-proof your career in the age of AI underscores the necessity of proactive adaptation and continuous learning. As AI reshapes industries and job roles, embracing these changes and equipping yourself with the necessary skills and knowledge is crucial. By fostering a deep understanding of AI, committing to ethical practices, and engaging in lifelong learning, you can navigate the transformations brought by AI, turning potential challenges into opportunities for growth and innovation. As we move forward, the next chapter will investigate emerging trends in AI, providing a glimpse into the future of this dynamic field and its potential to transform our world further.

13. THE NEXT FRONTIER: EMERGING TRENDS IN AI

Any sufficiently advanced technology is indistinguishable from magic.[1]

— ARTHUR CLARKE

Clarke's notion of advanced technology as a form of magic illuminates how AI transcends traditional boundaries, creating experiences and capabilities that once seemed unimaginable. From dynamic, self-adapting digital environments to the integration of AI with quantum computing, we are not just observing technology's evolution but participating in a revolution that redefines our interaction with the digital world.

Imagine stepping into an art gallery where the paintings shift and transform before your eyes, adapting and responding to your movements and emotions. This is not just a fantasy but a glimpse into what the next generation of AI models is beginning to enable in real-

1. Clarke, A. C. (1962). *Profiles of the Future: An Inquiry into the Limits of the Possible*. Harper & Row.

world applications. As we advance beyond the digital confines of text and image generation, AI is poised to redefine our interactions with technology, making digital environments more dynamic, immersive, and intuitively responsive than ever before. This chapter explores the frontiers AI pushes, from enhancing 3D modeling and virtual reality to creating interactive digital environments that react and evolve based on user input.

BEYOND TEXT AND IMAGES: THE NEXT GENERATION OF AI MODELS

The evolution of AI has reached a pivotal juncture where its capabilities extend far beyond generating text and static images. The next generation of AI models is venturing into uncharted territories, such as sophisticated 3D modeling and profoundly immersive virtual reality experiences, which were once the exclusive domain of human experts. These advanced models enhance digital creations' aesthetic and functional aspects and transform how we interact with machines and digital interfaces.

Expanding AI's Creative Horizons

AI's 3-D modeling and virtual reality exploration signifies a significant leap in creative and functional capabilities. For instance, in the architectural and entertainment industries, AI-driven tools are now being used to generate complex 3D models that can be adjusted in real-time, allowing for rapid prototyping and iterative design processes that were previously unthinkable. This capability enables architects and designers to experiment with different configurations at a pace and scale that accelerates innovation and efficiency.

AI in 3D Modeling and Virtual Reality

In virtual reality, AI is crucial in crafting visually stunning environments that can interact with users in a deeply personalized way. Imagine a virtual training module for medical students developed using AI that reacts to the students' decisions in real-time, providing a dynamic learning environment that adapts to their educational needs. Such applications underscore AI's potential to enhance the learning experience by simulating complex, real-world scenarios that respond and evolve according to user inputs.

Interactivity and AI

Interactivity is where AI's potential truly comes to life. By integrating AI with interactive technologies, digital environments can become more responsive, providing users with experiences tailored to their preferences and actions. For example, AI can analyze a user's interactions in a digital environment to predict and prepare contextually appropriate responses, enhancing the user's engagement and immersion. This level of interactivity has profound implications for fields ranging from education to entertainment and beyond, where personalized experiences can significantly enhance effectiveness and satisfaction.

Ethical and Technical Challenges

However, with great potential comes significant responsibility. The advancement of AI in creating interactive and adaptive digital environments also brings forth complex ethical and technical challenges. One of the primary issues is privacy: as AI requires enormous amounts of data to learn and adapt, ensuring the confidentiality and security of user data becomes paramount. Furthermore, the autonomy of AI-driven systems raises questions about control and decision-making in critical scenarios, necessitating robust ethical frameworks and governance to ensure these systems are used responsibly.

As we explore these new frontiers, it becomes increasingly clear that the next generation of AI models offers unprecedented opportunities to enhance and enrich our interactions with digital worlds. The key to unlocking these opportunities lies in our ability to harness AI's potential responsibly, ensuring that we do so with a careful blend of innovation and ethical consideration as we step into these new frontiers.

AI IN DECENTRALIZED NETWORKS: BLOCKCHAIN AND BEYOND

In the evolving technology, the convergence of AI and blockchain enables a new era of secure and decentralized digital solutions. This synergy is a technological advancement and a fundamental shift in how data is managed, processed, and utilized across various sectors. As you explore this intersection, it's crucial to understand how these technologies complement each other, creating systems that are efficient and inherently resistant to fraud and breaches, thereby enhancing trust and security in digital transactions.

AI and Blockchain Synergies

Integrating AI and blockchain technologies is revolutionizing how we think about data security and business processes. Blockchain provides an immutable and transparent decentralized ledger, making it an optimal platform for storing sensitive data that AI systems can analyze and learn from without risks of tampering or unauthorized access. For instance, in supply chain management, AI can predict and optimize logistics while blockchain securely tracks the authenticity and movement of goods. This combination ensures that AI decisions are based on accurate and secure data, enhancing overall business efficiency and reliability.

Moreover, AI can enhance blockchain's capabilities by introducing automated smart contracts that are self-executing and self-adapting based on real-time data and outcomes. This means that these contracts can update their protocols without human intervention based on criteria learned and analyzed by AI. Such advancements are particularly transformative in the real estate and finance sectors, where contract agility and accuracy are paramount. AI's ability to analyze boundless amounts of data can lead to more nuanced and context-aware intelligent contracts, further strengthening the trust in blockchain's decentralized transactions.

Decentralized AI Marketplaces

The rise of decentralized AI marketplaces represents a significant shift in how data and AI services are exchanged. Traditional models often rely on centralized platforms where data exchange and AI model training occur on a single server or within a limited network, posing risks related to data privacy and single points of failure. Decentralized AI marketplaces, however, leverage blockchain to create a distributed ecosystem where individuals and organizations can securely share data and access AI services without relying on a central authority.

These marketplaces enable users to contribute their data, participate in model training, or even share proprietary AI algorithms, all while ensuring that their intellectual property is protected through blockchain's secure, traceable transactions. For example, a healthcare provider could contribute anonymized patient data to a decentralized marketplace where AI developers can train diagnostic models. Other healthcare providers can access or purchase the resulting models, with transactions and contributions recorded transparently on the blockchain. This not only accelerates AI development by providing access to diverse datasets but also democratizes AI by lowering barriers to entry for smaller players who can now contribute to and benefit from collective AI advancements.

Enhancing Security with AI

AI's role in enhancing the security of blockchain networks is multifaceted. Through continuous monitoring and analysis of blockchain transactions, AI can detect patterns indicative of fraudulent activities or potential security breaches. These capabilities are crucial in preempting attacks and addressing vulnerabilities in real time. AI-driven security protocols can automatically update themselves to counter new threats, a level of responsiveness critical in today's fast-evolving threat scenarios.

Moreover, AI can optimize the performance of blockchain networks by predicting bottlenecks and suggesting improvements in data throughput and transaction processing. This enhances the efficiency of blockchain networks and ensures that they can process large volumes of transactions securely and swiftly, which is crucial for scalability in applications like digital payments and identity verification.

Challenges in Decentralization

While integrating AI with decentralized technologies offers numerous benefits but presents unique challenges. Technical hurdles, such as ensuring the compatibility of AI algorithms with decentralized architectures, can take time and effort. AI systems require substantial computational resources for data processing and learning, which can be challenging to manage in a decentralized environment typically characterized by limited processing capabilities on individual nodes.

Ethically, the decentralization of AI raises questions about accountability and control. As decision-making processes become more automated and distributed, determining responsibility for the outcomes of AI-driven decisions becomes complex. Ensuring fairness and transparency in these systems is crucial, mainly in critical applications such as legal adjudication or healthcare.

As we move forward, the fusion of AI and blockchain promises to transform industries by providing secure, transparent, and efficient solutions. However, realizing this potential fully requires continuous technological innovation and regulatory and ethical frameworks that guide the development and deployment of these transformative tools.

THE ROLE OF QUANTUM COMPUTING IN FUTURE AI DEVELOPMENTS

Quantum computing enables an incredible leap forward in our capability to process information, starkly contrasting the classical computing models that have powered the previous generations of AI developments. At its core, quantum computing harnesses the phenomena of quantum mechanics to process computations at speeds previously unattainable by traditional computers, using what are known as quantum bits or qubits. Unlike classical bits, representing data as either zeroes or ones, qubits can exist simultaneously in many states because of the superposition principle. This ability allows quantum computers to handle vast datasets and perform complex calculations much more efficiently than their classical counterparts. For you, as someone curious about the future of technology, understanding quantum computing is akin to looking at a new dimension where the rules of the game are fundamentally different and far more potent.

Accelerating AI with Quantum Computing

Integrating quantum computing into AI is poised to revolutionize how machines learn, interpret, and interact with data. Quantum algorithms have the potential to drastically reduce the time required for dataset processing and model training phases in machine learning. This acceleration is not just incremental; it's transformative, enabling AI to tackle more complex, nuanced problems at speeds that today's AI can't match. For instance, in scenarios involving real-time data processing, such as autonomous vehicle navigation or high-frequency trading, quantum-enhanced AI could analyze and react to new information instantaneously, surpassing current AI systems' capabilities. This speed and the ability to handle multi-dimensional data opens new horizons for AI applications previously constrained by computational limitations.

Quantum AI Applications

The applications of quantum-enhanced AI are as varied as they are impactful. In the field of cryptography, quantum computing introduces both challenges and solutions. It poses a significant threat to traditional encryption methods, as its capability to quickly factor large numbers can break many of the cryptographic protocols that secure our digital communications. However, this same power can be harnessed to develop new, virtually unbreakable encryption techniques, often called quantum cryptography. In drug discovery, quantum AI can analyze the potential interactions between millions of molecules and human biology much faster than current methods, significantly speeding up the development of new drugs and therapies. Moreover, in optimization problems central to logistics and operations across industries, quantum AI can find the most efficient routes or strategies that minimize costs and time, transforming sectors like manufacturing and supply chain management.

However, this same power can be harnessed to develop new, virtually unbreakable encryption techniques, often called quantum cryptography. In drug discovery, quantum AI can analyze the potential interactions between millions of molecules and human biology much faster than current methods, significantly speeding up the development of new drugs and therapies. Moreover, in optimization problems central to logistics and operations across industries, quantum AI can find the most efficient routes or strategies that minimize costs and time, transforming sectors like manufacturing and supply chain management.

Preparing for the Quantum AI Era

As we stand on the brink of the quantum AI era, individuals and businesses must begin preparing for the seismic changes these technologies are expected to bring. For professionals in AI and computing, continuous education on quantum theory and its applications in AI will be essential. Universities and online platforms increasingly offer courses and certifications in quantum computing that can provide foundational knowledge and skills. For businesses, particularly those relying heavily on data security, logistics, or complex system optimizations, beginning to explore quantum computing partnerships and investments will be a strategic move. Engaging with technology providers and quantum computing startups can offer insights into how quantum AI could specifically benefit your operations and what infrastructural adjustments will be necessary to integrate these advanced systems.

As we continue to explore AI's potential, integrating quantum computing into this field promises enhanced capabilities and a fundamental shift in the problems we can solve. The quantum AI era will challenge our current understanding of data processing and machine learning, heralding a future where AI's speed and intelligence could surpass what was once considered science fiction.

BRIDGING THE HUMAN-AI COLLABORATION GAP

As we advance into an era profoundly shaped by artificial intelligence, the interaction between humans and AI systems becomes a critical area of focus. The essence of this interaction is not about allowing AI to take over human roles but rather enhancing and extending human capabilities. Effective collaboration between humans and AI hinges on designing systems and strategies that improve mutual understanding and complementarity. This approach augments both parties' efficiency and fosters a symbiotic relationship where each can learn from the other, leading to continuous improvement and innovation.

Enhancing Human-AI Interaction

One of the most effective strategies for improving human-AI interaction is implementing user-friendly interfaces that facilitate more transparent communication between human users and AI systems. This involves the development of intuitive dashboards and tools that allow users to monitor AI processes easily, understand decision-making pathways, and intervene when necessary. For instance, in a clinical setting, an AI system designed to support diagnostic processes should explain its diagnostic suggestions easily to medical professionals, enabling them to make informed decisions about patient care.

Moreover, integrating AI systems with natural language processing capabilities that can interpret and respond to human language in a contextually relevant manner can significantly enhance interaction. This not only makes AI systems more accessible to non-specialist users but also allows for more natural and efficient collaboration. Training AI systems in the subtleties of human communication and providing them with the ability to detect nuances can lead to smoother interactions and more effective collaborations.

AI as a Complement to Human Skills

The true potential of AI lies in its ability to complement human skills, thereby creating a workforce that is more capable than humans or machines alone. In creative industries, for example, AI can handle time-intensive tasks such as data analysis and pattern recognition, freeing human creatives to focus on the more subjective aspects of their work, like design and storytelling. This synergy allows for a higher level of creativity and productivity than could be achieved by humans or AI in isolation.

In sectors such as healthcare, AI's ability to quickly process and analyze significant amounts of medical data can assist doctors in making faster, more accurate diagnoses. However, patient care's empathetic and intuitive aspects remain distinctly human. Here, AI is a tool that enhances the doctor's capabilities but still needs to replace the human touch, which is crucial to patient care.

Trust and Transparency in AI Systems

Building trust in AI systems is paramount for fostering effective collaboration between humans and AI. Establishing this trust hinges on the principle of transparency, which necessitates that AI systems are engineered to offer clear, comprehensible insights into how they operate and make decisions. Consider, for example, an AI system deployed for financial forecasting. It should not only delineate the factors that guide its predictions but also clarify the level of confidence it attaches to these forecasts. By demystifying its decision-making process, such an AI system empowers users with the knowledge to make well-informed decisions, leveraging AI-generated insights with a clear understanding of their underlying logic.

The importance of transparency extends beyond mere operational insight; it also involves explaining the limitations and potential biases inherent in AI systems. Acknowledging these aspects helps users critically assess the reliability of AI insights and understand the contexts in which these systems can be most effectively employed. In parallel with transparency, implementing stringent security protocols is critical in sustaining trust in AI collaborations. Users must be assured of the integrity and confidentiality of their data when interacting with AI systems. This involves adopting state-of-the-art security measures to ensure against unauthorized access, data breaches, and other cyber threats. Moreover, AI systems must adhere to ethical guidelines and regulatory standards concerning data privacy, providing user information is processed and stored with the utmost respect for privacy rights. Together, transparency and robust security measures lay the foundation for a trust-based relationship between humans and AI, facilitating a collaborative environment where AI systems are viewed not as opaque, inscrutable entities but as reliable and comprehensible partners in innovation.

Future of Work with AI

Looking ahead, the integration of AI into the workplace is poised to significantly transform job roles and introduce novel dynamics within team structures. AI's role as a collaborative partner is expected to be pivotal, with its application spanning various sectors. In the legal field, AI could revolutionize how research is conducted, sifting through vast amounts of legal documents in a fraction of the time it would take a human. This could enable lawyers to focus more on strategy and client relationships. AI can customize learning experiences to individual student needs, enhancing the educational process and outcomes.

As AI systems take over more routine, repetitive, and data-intensive tasks, human workers must pivot towards roles that leverage their unique human skills. These include complex problem-solving, creative thinking, and advanced interpersonal skills—traits that AI is far from replicating. This shift will likely encourage a more fulfilling work environment where creativity and innovation are at the forefront and mundane tasks are automated. Integrating AI into various facets of life and work emphasizes the importance of designing AI systems that do not merely automate tasks but significantly enhance and complement human capabilities. The overarching goal is to foster a symbiotic relationship between humans and AI, where each plays to their strengths, leading to unprecedented efficiency and innovation. The future of AI in the workplace and society is not about replacing humans but about forming a powerful partnership and collaboration. This promises a future where AI is a force multiplier for human potential, enabling us to achieve more extraordinary accomplishments together.

LIFELONG LEARNING IN THE AGE OF AI

In an age where technological advancement accelerates with each passing day, Generative AI is a beacon of transformative potential, reshaping industries and personal lives. As you stand on the precipice of this technological renaissance, adapting and thriving in a world continuously reshaped by intelligent machines is essential. This section empowers you, the reader, with the knowledge and tools needed to navigate the future confidently. AI will not be a distant marvel but a present reality in the future.

Skill Development for the Future

Specific skills emerge as particularly valuable in the context of an AI-infused future. Critical thinking, for instance, allows you to navigate the vast amounts of information AI technologies can provide to make reasoned decisions. Creativity once thought to be the exclusive domain of humans, is now an essential skill in collaborating with AI, especially in fields like design, content creation, and problem-solving. Moreover, interdisciplinary knowledge—combining insights from various fields—enhances your ability to innovate and apply AI technologies effectively across different sectors. For example, understanding machine learning principles and environmental science can position you to tackle climate change more effectively by employing AI in novel ways.

Resources for Learning

Fortunately, the resources to facilitate this learning are more accessible than ever. Numerous online platforms offer courses tailored to all levels of proficiency. Websites like Coursera and edX, partnering with top universities, provide courses on everything from basic programming to advanced AI techniques. Community workshops and local seminars can offer hands-on experience and personalized guidance for those who prefer a more structured environment. Additionally, digital libraries and publications from institutions like IEEE and ACM are invaluable resources for further examining AI's technical aspects.

Cultivating an Adaptive Mindset

Adapting to a world where AI plays a central role requires more than just learning new skills—it demands a shift in mindset. Embracing change, viewing challenges as opportunities for growth, and maintaining curiosity are all facets of an adaptive mindset. This mindset can be cultivated through reflective journaling, which helps you become more conscious of your learning and growth patterns and stay engaged with a community of learners, which can support and inspire perseverance.

Additionally, developing soft skills such as leadership, communication, and ethical reasoning will become increasingly important as you navigate the complexities of a workplace augmented by AI.

ETHICAL CONSIDERATIONS FOR FUTURE AI TECHNOLOGIES

In Generative AI, the ethical frameworks guiding its development and application require continuous adaptation and refinement to meet the issues posed by new technologies and societal shifts. The quick pace at which AI evolution can outstrip the current ethical guidelines that govern them leads to scenarios where innovation overshadows ethical considerations. To address this, ethical frameworks must evolve concurrently with technological advancements, ensuring that each new iteration of AI technology is developed and implemented responsibly.

Global Ethical Standards

Establishing global ethical standards for AI is another critical area of focus. As AI technologies do not recognize national borders, their impact is global. However, creating ethical standards that are both globally applicable and respectful of cultural diversity is challenging. Different cultures have varying expectations and norms regarding privacy, autonomy, and the role of technology, which can lead to conflicting views on what constitutes ethical AI. For example, surveillance technologies powered by AI may be more acceptable in some societies than others, leading to international tensions and challenges in deploying these technologies globally.

To navigate these challenges, international bodies and organizations must play a key role in bringing diverse cultural perspectives together to establish a set of core principles that respect universal rights while allowing for local variations in implementation. This requires a concerted effort from nations, corporations, and civil societies to engage in dialogue and collaboration to find common ground on critical ethical issues. Developing these standards should be an inclusive process that considers the perspectives of technologists and ethicists and includes input from the broader public to ensure that AI development aligns with societal values and needs.

Transparency and Accountability

Transparency in AI algorithms and accountability for AI-driven decisions remain paramount as AI systems become more integrated into critical aspects of society. Transparency makes the workings of AI systems understandable to users and stakeholders, which is essential for building trust and enabling effective oversight. For AI systems involved in decision-making processes, stakeholders must understand how decisions are made, what data is used, and the reasoning behind these decisions. This transparency allows users to challenge or seek redress for decisions that may affect them adversely.

Accountability in AI involves establishing clear guidelines on the responsible party for the decisions made by AI systems and ensuring that these systems operate within established legal and ethical boundaries. As AI systems are designed and deployed by human agents, these agents must ultimately be held accountable for the system's behavior. This accountability is crucial not only for legal and ethical reasons but also for fostering public trust in AI technologies.

Public Participation in AI Ethics

Advocating for increased public understanding and participation in discussions about AI ethics is essential for ensuring that AI development is aligned with public values and needs. Public participation helps demystify AI technologies and dispel myths and fears surrounding AI. By engaging the public in discussions about AI ethics, developers and policymakers can gain valuable insights into users' expectations and concerns, which can guide more responsible AI development. Public forums, consultations, and educational campaigns can effectively involve the public in these discussions.

Moreover, increasing public participation in AI ethics discussions ensures that diverse perspectives are heard, particularly from groups that may be disproportionately affected by AI technologies. This inclusivity strengthens the ethical frameworks around AI, as they are built on expert knowledge and a broad consensus among those who will live with AI's impacts.

As we forge ahead in exploring AI's possibilities, these considerations form the bedrock upon which responsible and beneficial AI development must be built. Ensuring that AI serves the common good while respecting individual rights and cultural diversity requires ongoing vigilance, collaboration, and commitment to ethical principles.

ADVOCATING FOR RESPONSIBLE AI DEVELOPMENT AND POLICY

The interplay between policy, regulation, and innovation forms a critical nexus that determines the trajectory of AI development and its alignment with public interest and ethical norms. As Generative AI technologies become increasingly embedded in every aspect of our lives, from education to finance, the imperative for robust policy frameworks that guide responsible development and deployment cannot be overstated. These frameworks ensure that AI technologies enhance societal well-being without infringing privacy, autonomy, or equity.

Role of Policy in Shaping AI

Policies and legislation are crucial in shaping the development of AI technologies. They set the boundaries within which innovation occurs, ensuring that advancements in AI are matched with considerations for safety, ethics, and public welfare. Effective policymaking in AI requires a proactive approach, anticipating future developments and potential challenges rather than merely reacting to them. For instance, policies regulating data use in AI can prevent abuses such as unwarranted surveillance and discrimination while fostering public trust in AI applications. Moreover, regulations can drive innovation by challenging AI developers to meet high safety and ethical responsibility standards.

Engaging with Policymakers

For individuals concerned about AI's ethical and societal implications, engaging with policymakers is a crucial step toward influencing how AI is governed. By voicing concerns, suggesting improvements, and advocating for ethical practices, you can contribute to shaping policies that govern AI development. This engagement can take various forms, from participating in public consultations and legislative hearings to more direct interactions with representatives and regulatory bodies. By staying informed about policy proposals and legislative developments in AI, you can more effectively advocate for policies that ensure AI technologies are developed and used in beneficial and just ways.

Encouragingly, many policymakers are increasingly aware of the complexities associated with AI and are open to input from experts, industry stakeholders, and the public. Your involvement can ensure that diverse perspectives are considered when creating AI policies, leading to more comprehensive and effective regulations. For example, by advocating for transparency in AI decision-making processes, you can help ensure that AI systems are accountable and that their operations are understandable. This is essential for building trust and acceptance among users.

Industry Standards and Self-Regulation

While government policies play a critical role in regulating AI, the industry also significantly shapes ethical AI development through standards and self-regulation. Industry standards often address specific technical and ethical issues more swiftly than legislative processes, adapting quickly to new technological developments. These standards, developed collaboratively by experts across the field, provide guidelines that help companies implement ethical practices in AI development and use.

When done responsibly, self-regulation can complement governmental regulations, filling gaps and offering more granular guidance tailored to specific technologies and applications. For instance, tech companies can adopt ethical codes of conduct that outline commitments to fairness, non-discrimination, and transparency, even in areas not yet covered by formal regulations. However, more than relying on self-regulation is required with oversight. Independent bodies must rigorously audit and enforce these self-regulatory measures to effectively prevent conflicts of interest and guarantee that companies adhere to their ethical declarations.

Building an Informed Public

Educating the public about AI technologies and their societal implications is fundamental to fostering an informed debate about AI ethics and policy. Understanding AI can demystify the technology, dispel unfounded fears, and enable individuals to make informed decisions about their interactions with AI systems. Educational initiatives can range from integrating AI topics into school curricula to organizing community seminars and creating online resources that make learning about AI accessible.

An informed public is empowered to discuss AI regulation and advocate for responsible AI development. By understanding AI's potential and risks, individuals can more effectively participate in dialogues shaping AI's ethical environment, advocating for technologies that align with societal values and contribute positively to the common good.

As we conclude our discussion on the next frontiers in AI, we reflect on the collective responsibility shared by policymakers, industry leaders, and the public in steering the development of AI toward a future that upholds ethical standards and promotes the well-being of all. The conversations and actions we undertake today in advocating for responsible AI will shape the legacy of this transformative technology for generations to come.

KEEP THE CONVERSATION ALIVE!

The capabilities of AI are constantly evolving, and so too must our understanding of it. Keep the conversation going so that we can learn from each other and make the best use of this revolutionary tool. You can start right now!

Simply by sharing your honest opinion of this book and a little about how it has changed your understanding, you'll play an important part in the ongoing conversation and help new readers unlock the potential of generative AI.

Thank you so much for your support. We have an exciting future ahead of us, and I can't wait to see what's in store for us!

Scan the QR code below

Conclusion

As we conclude our explorative adventure into Generative AI, it's clear that we've only scratched the surface of its potential to redefine industries, augment our daily creative endeavors, and enhance decision-making capabilities. This adventure has unfolded the layers of technology at the brink of reshaping professions and the nuances of our daily existence.

From the beginning, I intended to peel away the veil of complexity surrounding Generative AI to present it as a readily accessible tool far exceeding the confines of high-tech circles. This book has equipped you with the knowledge and confidence to embrace Generative AI as an integral component of your toolkit, regardless of your professional or personal background.

Through our discussions, we've come to appreciate Generative AI as more than a mere conduit for automating tasks; it emerges as a beacon of innovation. Its capability to extend the boundaries of what machines are capable of, in synergy with human creativity and insight, appears boundless. However, with great power comes great responsibility. We have deliberated on the ethical considerations essential for its application—advocating for ethical usage, inclusivity, and conscientious deployment to guarantee that its advantages reach all corners of society equitably.

Diving into the world of Generative AI is an invitation to a perpetual cycle of learning and evolution, prompting you to play an active role in shaping its development. Whether you're a creator, a consumer, or a curious mind, your engagement with AI can significantly influence its integration into our society.

I am thrilled to offer an exclusive bonus to facilitate further this adventure: a meticulously curated collection of Generative AI prompts. These prompts ignite your creative spirit and foster experimentation, acting as practical launchpads for your ventures. They serve as a bridge, translating the insights from this book into tangible actions, whether your interest lies in writing, designing, or pioneering innovations.

Step into a dynamic community of AI enthusiasts, scholars, and ethicists, where your perspectives and inquiries contribute to the ongoing conversation about Generative AI. Remember, every interaction, irrespective of its scale, enriches our collective understanding and fosters a responsible framework for the future of AI.

In conclusion, we view it not as an endpoint but as the beginning of a continuous exploration and dialogue with technology. Let's persist in learning, sharing, and innovating to ensure that AI is a benevolent force equipped to embellish our world for future generations.

Thank you for accompanying me on this adventure. I am keen to discover how you will apply these newfound insights to your personal and professional lives, and I eagerly anticipate your stories and feedback. Let us maintain this dialogue and work together to ensure that our collective future with AI is as enlightened as it is promising.

RESOURCES

1. Pro Epic Technology Solutions. (n.d.). General - Artificial intelligence. Retrieved from https://www.pro-epic.com/blog/glossary/artificial-intelligence.html

2. Aquino, G. (2023). Explaining and visualizing embeddings of one-dimensional convolutional models in human activity recognition tasks. *Sensors, 23*(9), 4409. https://doi.org/10.3390/s23094409

3. Vestrics. (n.d.). Artificial intelligence & machine learning. Retrieved from https://www.vestrics.in/artificial-intelligence-machine-learning/

4. Techno Station. (n.d.). Why are machine learning tools becoming popular in tech? Here are the details. Retrieved from https://www.technostation.com/why-are-machine-learning-tools-becoming-popular-in-tech-here-are-the-details/

5. Adeak. (n.d.). What does 'Generative adversarial network' mean in AI? Retrieved from https://www.adeak.com/what-does-generative-adversarial-network-mean-in-ai/

6. Zeng, D., Dai, Y., Li, F., Sherratt, R. S., & Wang, J. (2018). Adversarial learning for distant supervised relation extraction. *Computational Materials Communications, 55*, 121. https://doi.org/10.3970/cmc.2018.055.121

7. Editor and Publisher. (n.d.). Harnessing AI power, the new frontier for news media executives. Retrieved from https://www.editorandpublisher.com/stories/harnessing-ai-power,244601

8. EZ Newswire. (n.d.). Peel Away Labs enters distribution agreement with Medline. Retrieved from https://app.eznewswire.com/news/peel-away-labs-enters-distribution-agreement-with-medline

9. Aquino, G. (2023). Explaining and Visualizing Embeddings of One-Dimensional Convolutional Models in Human Activity Recognition Tasks. Sensors, 23(9), 4409.

10. Trending Webblogg. (2023, August). Retrieved from https://trending.webblogg.se/2023/august/

11. MIT News. (n.d.). Explained: Generative AI. Retrieved from https://www.techtarget.com/searchenterpriseai/definition/generative-AI

12. CMSWire. (n.d.). Generative AI Timeline: 9 Decades of Notable Milestones. Retrieved from https://www.cmswire.com/digital-experience/generative-ai-timeline-9-decades-of-notable-milestones/

13. Marr, B. (2023, July 24). The Difference Between Generative AI And Traditional AI. Forbes. Retrieved from https://www.forbes.com/sites/bernardmarr/2023/07/24/the-difference-between-generative-ai-and-traditional-ai-an-easy-explanation-for-anyone/

14. AIMultiple. (2024). Top 100+ Generative AI Applications / Use Cases in 2024. Retrieved from https://research.aimultiple.com/generative-ai-applications/

15. IBM. (n.d.). What is a Neural Network? Retrieved from https://www.ibm.com/topics/neural-networks

16. Sciotex. (n.d.). CNN vs GAN: A Comparative Analysis in Image Processing for Computer Vision Systems. Retrieved from https://sciotex.com/cnn-vs-gan-a-comparative-analysis-in-image-processing-for-computer-vision-systems/

17. Algotive. (n.d.). The History of Artificial Intelligence, Machine Learning and Deep Learning. Retrieved from https://www.algotive.ai/blog/the-history-of-artificial-intelligence-machine-learning-and-deep-learning

18. Packt Publishing. (n.d.). Generative AI in Natural Language Processing. Retrieved from https://www.packtpub.com/article-hub/generative-ai-in-natural-language-processing

19. Dorin, A., & McCormack, J. (2023). Generative artificial intelligence, human creativity, and art. *PNAS Nexus, 3*(3), pga e052. https://academic.oup.com/pnasnexus/article/3/3/pgae052/7618478

20. Gregorio, N. (2023, November 13). Generative AI and the art of personalization. *Forbes*. https://www.forbes.com/sites/forbestechcouncil/2023/11/13/generative-ai-and-the-art-of-personalization/

21. Innodata. (n.d.). Generative AI in drug discovery: How AI is transforming pharma. https://innodata.com/generative-ai-in-drug-discovery-how-ai-is-transforming-pharma/

22. Data Science Central. (n.d.). Ethical boundaries in generative AI: Human vs. machine. https://www.datasciencecentral.com/generative-ai-ethics-navigating-the-boundary-between-human-and-machine-creativity/

23. CXO | NXT - Unlocking the Creative Potential: Generative AI and its Role in Innovative Content Creation. https://cxonxt.com/news-feed/unlocking-the-creative-potential-generative-ai-and-its-role-in-innovative-content-creation/

24. Malik, T. (n.d.). Here's how generative AI is transforming retail. *Medium*. https://medium.com/all-things-work/the-rise-of-generative-ai-in-social-media-and-its-impact-on-the-future-of-gen-ai-c4bfeb232f47

25. Center for Strategic & International Studies. (n.d.). Navigating the risks of artificial intelligence on the digital news landscape. https://www.csis.org/analysis/navigating-risks-artificial-intelligence-digital-news-landscape

26. MediaList.info. (2024, January 7). How generative AI is redefining the world of smart home. https://medialist.info/en/2024/01/07/the-home-of-tomorrow-how-generative-ai-is-redefining-the-world-of-smart-home/

27. Kanerika. (n.d.). Generative AI risks and challenges. https://kanerika.com/blogs/generative-ai-risks-and-challenges/

28. McKinsey & Company. (n.d.). Boost your productivity with generative AI. https://www.mckinsey.com/featured-insights/future-of-work/ai-automation-and-the-future-of-work-ten-things-to-solve-for

29. Hurix Digital. (n.d.). How AI is personalizing education for every student. https://www.hurix.com/how-ai-is-personalizing-education-for-every-student/

30. Allard, J., Ring, M., & Ison, J. (2023). Generative artificial intelligence, human creativity, and art. *PNAS Nexus, 3*(3), pgae052. https://academic.oup.com/pnasnexus/article/3/3/pgae052/7618478

31. Clancy, T. (2023). The Rise of Ethical Concerns about AI Content Creation. *Computer Society.* https://www.computer.org/publications/tech-news/trends/ethical-concerns-on-ai-content-creation/

32. IBM Think Blog. (2023). Shedding light on AI bias with real world examples. https://www.ibm.com/blog/shedding-light-on-ai-bias-with-real-world-examples/

33. Securiti Team. (n.d.). Generative AI Privacy: Issues, Challenges & How to Protect? *Securiti Blog.* https://securiti.ai/generative-ai-privacy/

34. Gopinath, G. (2024). AI Will Transform the Global Economy. Let's Make Sure It Benefits Humanity. *IMF Blog.* https://www.imf.org/en/Blogs/Articles/2024/01/14/ai-will-transform-the-global-economy-lets-make-sure-it-benefits-humanity

35. Jain, A. (2023). Governing Ethical AI: Rules & Regulations Preventing Unethical AI. *Analytics Vidhya.* https://www.analyticsvidhya.com/blog/2023/01/governing-ethical-ai-rules-regulations-preventing-unethical-ai/

36. Techopedia Staff. (n.d.). 10 Free Generative AI Tools That Are Great for Beginners. *Techopedia.* https://www.techopedia.com/6-free-generative-ai-tools-that-are-great-for-beginners

37. Software Advice. (2024). Best Generative AI Software - 2024 Reviews & Pricing. https://www.softwareadvice.com/generative-ai/

38. Rouse, M. (n.d.). 7 generative AI challenges that businesses should consider. *TechTarget.* https://www.techtarget.com/searchenterpriseai/tip/Generative-AI-challenges-that-businesses-should-consider

39. Aisera. (2024). Getting Started with Generative AI: Step by Step Guide [2024]. https://aisera.com/blog/start-with-generative-ai/

40. Agente Studio. (n.d.). *How to train a generative AI models.* https://agentestudio.com/blog/train-generative-ai-models

41. How VR can be used in medical education? - wi4.org. https://wi4.org/ufaq/how-vr-can-be-used-in-medical-education/

42. Shelf.io. (n.d.). *Fine-tuning LLMs for AI accuracy and effectiveness.* https://shelf.io/blog/fine-tuning-llms-for-ai-accuracy-and-effectiveness/

43. Helwan, A. (n.d.). *Recent advancements in GANs and style transfer.* https://abdulkaderhelwan.medium.com/recent-advancements-in-gans-and-style-transfer-b7ba2b54cc68

44. TechGig. (n.d.). *5 online AI communities that every AI enthusiast should know about.* https://cio.techgig.com/social-media/5-online-ai-communities-that-every-ai-enthusiast-should-know-about/articleshow_b2b/76393631.cms

45. Transcend. (n.d.). *Key principles for ethical AI development.* https://transcend.io/blog/ai-ethics

46. Brookings. (n.d.). *Algorithmic bias detection and mitigation: Best practices and policies to reduce consumer harms.* https://www.brookings.edu/articles/algorithmic-bias-detection-and-mitigation-best-practices-and-policies-to-reduce-consumer-harms/

47. BigID. (n.d.). *8 generative AI best practices for privacy.* https://bigid.com/blog/8-generative-ai-best-practices-for-privacy/

48. Wertz, J. (2023, November 19). *How AI can be leveraged for diversity and inclusion.* Forbes. https://www.forbes.com/sites/jiawertz/2023/11/19/how-ai-can-be-leveraged-for-diversity-and-inclusion/

49. Talespin. (n.d.). *The power of generative AI in VR: A gateway to innovation.* https://www.talespin.com/reading/the-power-of-generative-ai-in-vr-a-gateway-to-innovation

50. McKinsey & Company. (n.d.). *Generative AI in energy and materials.* https://www.mckinsey.com/industries/metals-and-mining/our-insights/beyond-the-hype-new-opportunities-for-gen-ai-in-energy-and-materials

51. Marr, B. (2024, March 5). The future of generative AI: 6 predictions everyone should know about. Forbes. https://www.forbes.com/sites/bernardmarr/2024/03/05/the-future-of-generative-ai-6-predictions-everyone-should-know-about/

52. Forbes Tech Council. (2023, October 17). Which ethical implications of generative AI should companies focus on? Forbes. https://www.forbes.com/sites/forbestechcouncil/2023/10/17/which-ethical-implications-of-generative-ai-should-companies-focus-on/

53. Google Cloud Team. (n.d.). Building the most open and innovative AI ecosystem. Google Cloud. Retrieved May 10, 2024, from https://cloud.google.com/blog/products/ai-machine-learning/building-an-open-generative-ai-partner-ecosystem

54. Ching-Cheng, S., & Der-Jen, L. (2020). Rural Tourism and Environmental Sustainability—A Study on a Model for Assessing the

Developmental Potential of Organic Agritourism. Sustainability, 12(22), 9642.

55. Generative AI in SEO: Revolutionizing Digital Marketing - TheeDigital. https://www.theedigital.com/blog/generative-ai-in-seo

56. Cacal, N. C. (n.d.). Unequal access to AI and its cultural implications. LinkedIn. Retrieved May 10, 2024, from https://www.linkedin.com/pulse/unequal-access-ai-its-cultural-implications-nicole-c-cacal-ouf1c

57. West, D. M., & Allen, J. R. (n.d.). Strengthening international cooperation on AI. Brookings Institution. Retrieved May 10, 2024, from https://www.brookings.edu/articles/strengthening-international-cooperation-on-ai/

58. Latest Posts on Network Security - CyOp Security. https://cyopsecurity.com/insights/tag/network-security/

59. Unite AI Team. (n.d.). AI bias & cultural stereotypes: Effects, limitations, & mitigation. Unite.AI. Retrieved May 10, 2024, from https://www.unite.ai/ai-bias-cultural-stereotypes-effects-limitations-mitigation/

60. Forbes Tech Council. (2024, March 26). Why lifelong learning is even more important in the AI era. Forbes. https://www.forbes.com/sites/forbestechcouncil/2024/03/26/why-lifelong-learning-is-even-more-important-in-the-ai-era/

61. UNESCO. (n.d.). Recommendation on the ethics of artificial intelligence. UNESCO. Retrieved May 10, 2024, from https://www.unesco.org/en/artificial-intelligence/recommendation-ethics

62. International Monetary Fund. (2024, March 22). The economic impacts and the regulation of AI: A review of the academic literature and policy implications. IMF Working Papers. https://www.imf.org/en/Publications/WP/Issues/2024/03/22/The-Economic-Impacts-and-the-Regulation-of-AI-A-Review-of-the-Academic-Literature-and-546645

63. AI4K-12 Initiative. (n.d.). List of resources. AI4K12. Retrieved May 10, 2024, from https://ai4k12.org/resources/list-of-resources/

64. Forbes Communications Council. (2023, April 3). Generative AI in marketing: 5 use cases. Forbes. https://www.forbes.com/sites/forbescommunicationscouncil/2023/04/03/generative-ai-in-marketing-5-use-cases/

65. Tran, B. X., Vu, G. T., Ha, G. H., Vuong, Q.-H., Ho, M.-T., Vuong, T.-T., ... Ho, R. C. (2020). Artificial intelligence and personalized medicine. Cancer Control, 27(1), 1073274820935117. https://www.ncbi.nlm.nih.gov/pmc/articles/PMC7580505/

66. The Evolution of Generative AI and Its Impact on Human Intelligence - I Am Tzar. https://iamtzar.com/the-evolution-of-generative-ai-and-its-impact-on-human-intelligence/

67. Dobrescu, A., & Liu, Y. (2021). AI-enabled adaptive learning systems: A systematic review. *Educational Technology Research and Development, 69*, 15-33. https://www.sciencedirect.com/science/article/pii/S2666920X21000114

68. Marr, B. (2023, October 5). Generative AI is revolutionizing music: The vision for democratizing creation. *Forbes.* https://www.forbes.com/sites/bernardmarr/2023/10/05/generative-ai-is-revolutionizing-music-loudlys-vision-for-democratizing-creation/

69. H. James Wilson, P. Daugherty, & N. Morini-Bianzino. (2018, July). Collaborative intelligence: Humans and AI are joining forces. *Harvard Business Review.* https://hbr.org/2018/07/collaborative-intelligence-humans-and-ai-are-joining-forces

70. CG Spectrum College of Digital Art & Animation. (n.d.). What is AI art and how will it impact artists? https://www.cgspectrum.com/blog/what-is-ai-art-how-will-it-impact-artists

71. Schatsky, D., & Schwartz, J. (2022, November). How generative AI is changing creative work. *Harvard Business Review.* https://hbr.org/2022/11/how-generative-ai-is-changing-creative-work

72. Gershgorn, D. (n.d.). The rise of ethical concerns about AI content creation. *IEEE Computer Society.* https://www.computer.org/publications/tech-news/trends/ethical-concerns-on-ai-content-creation/

73. How to create content with ChatGPT?. https://coinbae.org/how-to-create-content-with-chatgpt/

74. Princeton University. (n.d.). Case studies - Princeton dialogues on AI and ethics. https://aiethics.princeton.edu/case-studies/

75. Engels, R., & Grote, T. (2020, October). A practical guide to building ethical AI. *Harvard Business Review.* https://hbr.org/2020/10/a-practical-guide-to-building-ethical-ai

76. UNESCO. (n.d.). Ethics of artificial intelligence. https://www.unesco.org/en/artificial-intelligence/recommendation-ethics

77. Latest Posts on Network Security - CyOp Security. https://cyopsecurity.com/insights/tag/network-security/

78. Renjith, V. R., & Shyamasundar, R. K. (2022). Stakeholder roles in artificial intelligence projects. *Systems Research and Behavioral Science, 39*(3), 354-365. https://www.sciencedirect.com/science/article/pii/S266672152200028X

79. AI Universe Explorer. (n.d.). 29+ AI communities and forums for machine learning enthusiasts. https://aiuniverseexplorer.com/ai-communities/

80. SDxCentral. (n.d.). What is AI networking? Use cases, benefits, and challenges. https://www.sdxcentral.com/networking/definitions/what-is-ai-networking-use-cases-benefits-and-challenges/

81. (2020). Integrating Virtual Reality and GIS Tools for Geological Mapping, Data Collection and Analysis: An Example from the Metaxa Mine, Santorini (Greece). Applied Sciences, 10(23), 8317.

82. ABO Launches Patient Experience Survey-Based Quality Improvement Pilot. https://www.diplomatedigest.com/post/2017/05/05/abo-launches-patient-experience-survey-based-quality-improvement-pilot

83. Wang, Y., Liu, L., & Wang, C. (2023). Trends in using deep learning algorithms in biomedical prediction systems. Frontiers in Neuroscience.

84. Data Science Dojo. (n.d.). Top 9 AI conferences and events in USA - 2023. https://datasciencedojo.com/blog/ai-conferences-and-events-2023/

85. Coursera. (n.d.). How to learn artificial intelligence: A beginner's guide. https://www.coursera.org/articles/how-to-learn-artificial-intelligence

86. Kutun, B., & Schmidt, W. (2019). BPMN Wheel: Board Game for Business Process Modelling. European Conference on Games Based Learning, 1008-1012,XVIII.

87. Marr, B. (2024, March 21). The best generative AI tools transforming education. *Forbes*. https://www.forbes.com/sites/bernardmarr/2024/03/21/the-best-generative-ai-tools-transforming-education/

88. European Parliament. (2020). The ethics of artificial intelligence: Issues and initiatives. https://www.europarl.europa.eu/RegData/etudes/STUD/2020/634452/EPRS_STU(2020)634452_EN.pdf

89. Latest Posts on Network Security - CyOp Security. https://cyopsecurity.com/insights/tag/network-security/

90. IEEE Spectrum. (2023). Spectrum's Top AI Stories of 2023. Retrieved from https://spectrum.ieee.org/ai-news-2023

91. Top eCommerce Fraud Prevention Companies - Merchant Fraud Journal. https://www.merchantfraudjournal.com/top-ecommerce-fraud-protection-solutions/

92. Marr, B. (2024, March 21). The Best Generative AI Tools Transforming Education. Forbes. Retrieved from https://www.forbes.com/sites/bernardmarr/2024/03/21/the-best-generative-ai-tools-transforming-education/

93. Data Science Dojo. (2023). Top 9 AI conferences and events in USA - 2023. Retrieved from https://datasciencedojo.com/blog/ai-conferences-and-events-2023/

94. Hagerty, A., & Rubin, O. (2020, October). A Practical Guide to Building Ethical AI. Harvard Business Review. Retrieved from https://hbr.org/2020/10/a-practical-guide-to-building-ethical-ai

95. (2021). Comment on gi-2021-23. https://doi.org/10.5194/gi-2021-23-rc1

96. TechTarget. (n.d.). Generative AI Ethics: 8 Biggest Concerns and Risks. Retrieved from https://www.techtarget.com/searchenterpriseai/tip/Generative-AI-ethics-8-biggest-concerns

97. European Parliament Research Service. (2020). The ethics of artificial intelligence: Issues and initiatives (2020/634452). Retrieved from https://www.europarl.europa.eu/RegData/etudes/STUD/2020/634452/EPRS_STU(2020)634452_EN.pdf

98. Haight, Mysia. "55+ Quotes About Fear—of the Unknown, Change, Love, and More." Audible Blog. Last modified January 4, 2021. https://www.audible.com/blog/quotes-fear

Made in the USA
Middletown, DE
22 August 2024

59604693R00128